when
HEALING
doesn't
HAPPEN

Michele Neal

when
HEALING
doesn't
HAPPEN

A LIFE LIVED FOR GOD
THROUGH THE JOURNEY
OF SUFFERING

Dedication

I dedicate this book to God.

With every passing day, I know that I need Him more and more, and as you read this book, you will discover why.

To God be all the glory!

"And whatever you do, whether in word or deed, do it all in the name of the Lord Jesus, giving thanks to God the Father through him." – Colossians 3:17 NIV

"Whatever you do, work at it with all your heart, as working for the Lord, not for human masters, since you know that you will receive an inheritance from the Lord as a reward. It is the Lord Christ you are serving." – Colossians 3:23-24 NIV

Foreword

Michele has approached this all-important topic and burning issue, "When Healing Doesn't Happen" with great sensitivity and clarity. Using her own experience of long-term illness, she is able to work through deep issues in a meaningful and practical way. Having read Michele's previous books, as always, she meticulously backs up her insights with Scripture upon Scripture. Read with an open mind and receptive spirit, this book can be used of the Lord to strengthen both those with long-term health problems and seemingly unanswered prayer, as well as those acquainted with people who are experiencing this problem. My prayer is that this book will be a great blessing to many and that our Lord Jesus will mightily use it to His honour & glory.

– **Day Ashton** – Author of *Moments of Encouragement*, Freelance Writer and Bible Teacher, Blogger for *Day's Meditations* (daysmeditations.wordpress.com) and *In Defence of the Truth* (dayashtonuk.wixsite.com/indefenceofthetruth)

Acknowledgements

I would like to thank my wonderful husband, Chris, for once again helping me through the long haul of book writing. When I wrote the first one back in 2011, I thought that would be my lot. But the Lord compelled me to write a second book, then a third...and now a fourth! Thank you so much for putting up with me being hidden away in my office for half of your life! You are an amazing husband!

Thank you to my wonderful daughter, Emma, for taking on the challenge of proof reading the manuscript, spending many hours using your skills and offering your expert advice to get it all into shape. I knew that your gifting would come in handy one day, when I discovered you reading whole sentences from a children's book when you were only 3 years old! Your love for anything to do with books was evident at such a tender age!

Thank you to my sister Sharon, for encouraging me to write this book. You have known what it is like to go through long-term suffering, for many varied reasons, and when I said to you back in 2011 that this work was on my heart, you told me just how much a book was needed on this subject. I hope that what I have written will be like an oasis to the places in your soul that have become like dry wells during your own times in the 'wilderness of suffering'.

Thank you to the handful of like-minded brothers and sisters in Christ whom the Lord has brought into my life, who have encouraged and supported me in all the books I have written since 2011, and also to the many 'followers' around the world on Twitter, who have 'liked' and 're-tweeted' the things I have posted. Your companionship on this journey means a lot to me.

Thank you to four wonderful people who have taken time out of their busy lives to read my manuscript and write an endorsement – Day Ashton, Jennifer Rees Larcombe, Rev. Jack Munley, and Ruth Clemence. I appreciate immensely your support for this book, and I pray the Lord continues to bless you in all that you do for Him.

Finally, thank you to Jason Carter at JWC Creative, for your tireless work in getting this book published. Without your God-given gift, this book would still be just a document on my computer! Thank you so much Jason! God bless you!

Contents

A 'Withered Wisteria'
to a 'Beautiful Rose'!

As Michele's husband, I wanted to write something to give you a glimpse of who she is, and why she has written this book.

When Michele and I got together in 2005, she was a broken woman in almost every sense of the word. Her description of herself was that she felt like a 'withered wisteria'. I told her that somewhere along life's journey she would become a 'beautiful rose'!

Michele and I married in 2006. Whilst every couple's wedding day is unique, ours was different for one painful reason. When she held my arm as we walked down the aisle at the end of an amazingly spiritually-uplifting ceremony, it was because she felt so unwell and thought she was going to keel over. Our wedding day was full of joy, but it was marred with pain; the kind of pain that doesn't go away, despite whatever avenue of healing you have taken.

A room was booked at the wedding reception venue so that Michele could retire to it and rest as soon as we arrived there, whilst the wedding guests were enjoying themselves. Many people came up to me throughout the afternoon and evening with the same question, "Is Michele all right?" "Oh yes", I replied, "she is just resting…"

But the truth was very different. She was not 'all right' at all. Michele has been afflicted with the suffering of long-term physical pain all the time I have known her. In fact, it all began long before I ever met her, which she will share with you in this book.

Throughout our marriage I have learned to become a kind of 'buffer' between her and the outside world, especially during the mornings. Stress, noise, awkward people – these are all triggers for her physical symptoms. These factors can rapidly bring about pain of varying levels throughout her entire body. Sometimes she can barely function and needs to hide away in a quiet room for much of the day; other times she will be relatively sprightly from noon till bed-time.

I said I have become a kind of 'buffer' – I don't know the right word, but my role is that of protector, personal aide, 'interceptor.' What I mean is that I have to intercept phone calls and visitors to the home, intervene when people ask her lots of questions; there are a variety of subtle forms of 'attack' from which I need to protect her.

Life has been like this for all the 12 years that we have been married. During this time, Michele has experienced many good-intentioned people constantly checking that she has been prayed for; or recommending special retreats and healing centres, in the certain promise that God wants to heal her. Others explain that they are absolutely certain that **their** prayer, **right now**, will set her free 'in Jesus' name', but when nothing happens, they have looked at her with a somewhat bewildered expression.

Many of the individuals concerned are men and women of great faith, and I can relate to their heart's desire to see Michele healed. I fully understand their passion for miraculous healing, as this is very evident in the Bible.

But what if God doesn't bring about a miraculous healing in the lives of some who suffer with various ailments, illnesses, diseases or disabilities? Some will say, "But it is not God's will for **any** to suffer."

Michele is a born again, Spirit-filled, Bible-believing Christian, and in this book, you will read of her journey in Christ; a journey which has been marked with the burden of suffering; yet in all of this, her faith in God has strengthened, not weakened.

She is one of the most amazing, brave and strong people I have ever known. Most people who meet her have not the slightest idea that she is feeling unwell during the time they spend with her. I have often seen her chatting and being kind-hearted towards people while she is racked with pain. So often, I find myself imagining how I would cope, and the answer is I would simply crawl into my bed with a nice hot water bottle, and keep the world as far away from me as possible. When her pain level is bearable, Michele will often throw herself into 'doing' rather than resting, even though she feels unwell. On many occasions she will choose to clean the house, mow the lawns or dig up weeds; she tells me it keeps her mind off how she feels. Her ability to endure and overcome her life-long struggle always amazes me.

Despite all that she has endured on a daily basis, for so many years, I have watched God transform her from that 'withered wisteria' into a 'beautiful rose'. She still feels a great deal of physical pain, but she is no longer the broken woman that I met in 2005. She is now a vessel which God is using for His purposes, in spite of her suffering, as this book will reveal.

The reason Michele has written this book is to help the countless number of believers who struggle constantly with suffering of one kind or another, who may have felt 'falsely accused' by others of either not having enough faith for their healing, or not having confessed and repented of a particular sin, or sins. Whilst we know that these are valid reasons (as is unbelief) which can hinder healing from happening, I support Michele in what she writes; that any prayer for healing, which seems to go unanswered, is not necessarily due to these factors. For this reason, she has written this book to be a beacon of light, hope, comfort and encouragement for everyone who is travelling on the path of suffering.

So, with all this in mind, I commend this book to every believer who is struggling to understand the reasons for their continual suffering. I also commend it to those who may perhaps inadvertently be adding to the burdens of those whose healings haven't happened. It is my prayer that this book will give you a glimpse into the life of a long-term sufferer, and will encourage you to fully embrace the teaching of St. Paul, to bear one another's burden, and in so doing, fulfil the law of Christ (see Galatians 6:2).

Richest blessings in Christ Jesus.

Chris Neal

Introduction

The Reason for this Book

"Come to me, all you who are weary and burdened, and I will give you rest. Take my yoke upon you and learn from me, for I am gentle and humble in heart, and you will find rest for your souls."
Matthew 11:28-29 NIV

For about ten years, I have felt a deep compelling in my soul to write a book from a Christian perspective on the subject of 'When Healing Doesn't Happen'.

This book is the personal story of my life; a life lived for God through the journey of suffering. In the various chapters, I will share with you aspects of my life and my health before I gave my life to Christ in 1992, and will also share with you the journey I have travelled with Him and the things He has shown me for the 27 years that I have been one of His followers. It is not my intention with this book to do an in-depth study on suffering and healing, but simply to write of my journey.

To give you a glimpse before we get into the chapters, since becoming a follower of Christ, my life has had many ups and downs, with several times of being led by the Holy Spirit into the 'wilderness', where I have felt totally alone in the silence and pain, wondering why the Lord has taken me there. The issue of health and healing has been one of those long, dark times in the wilderness.

I have struggled with my health for as long as I can remember, and giving my life to Christ did not change the situation. Even 27 years of praying for God to heal me has not brought about what I have longed for. During this time, I have encountered indifference, insensitivity, and sometimes disdain towards my long-suffering from those **within** the Church, where I thought I would receive their grace and love. Sadly, I have discovered that many suffering Christians have experienced a similar response from those within the Church, and the result can be that those who suffer want to leave the Church and never step over the threshold ever again.

I am one who has resorted to this action, after an encounter with a fellow Christian who asked me how I was. This type of encounter was not the first I had experienced, but it was the one that had such an impact that it triggered something deep within me to write this book to try to help those who have felt wounded like this by the insensitive words of other Christians.

It has taken me until now to realise that many in the Church seem to have a 'quick fix' approach to the subject of suffering and healing, and towards believers who do not respond instantly to the 'name it, claim it' prayers of those who are held in esteem as having a 'special healing anointing' from the Lord.

The fact remains that many leaders, and even those who are not leaders, seem to not know what to do when they have prayed a healing prayer over a fellow Christian who has long-term chronic health conditions, and their prayer for that person has **not** resulted in them being miraculously healed. My experience has been that those who have not been healed after they have been prayed for, are treated with a measure of disdain, making them feel like they haven't been healed because they haven't got enough faith, or that there is some sin in their life which they aren't confessing. Yes, there may be situations where sin and unbelief could well be the reason, but taking this view towards all who suffer long-term conditions now seems to be approaching a default position. Those who continue to suffer, despite much prayer, are often left feeling isolated and avoided, causing them to feel like an outcast.

I have walked this painful path, and I am still walking on it to this day. It is my prayer that what I write in this book will resonate with many long-suffering Christians, and will give them a measure of comfort, hope and strength to endure in their own journey through the wilderness.

When healing doesn't happen, my many years of being a follower of Christ have taught me that God has a purpose in the pain. I encourage you to read on and join me on this journey of discovery...

Chapter 1

A Walk down 'Weary Lane' – A Snapshot of my Journey

"I am weary, O God; I am weary and worn out, O God."
Proverbs 30:1

'Weary Lane' is an apt description of the journey of my life for as long as I can remember. From the outside, no-one would really know how I am feeling on the **inside**. In my younger years I gained a Diploma in Beauty Therapy, and in view of how I felt physically, I made the most of how to apply natural-looking makeup to hide my pale and weary countenance.

When I am feeling well enough to attend evening church services, I spend some time doing my hair and makeup and putting on some nice clothes, and when most people see me, they say how well I look. I have got to the point in my journey where I simply respond with a "Thank you", because I am very aware that most people are not really interested in hearing about what it's like walking down 'Weary Lane'. If I do share anything, I discover that most people quickly want to change the subject, or hastily nip off to the loo to make their escape.

It's not that I want to bore people with the daily struggle of my life; it's just that, over the years, I have encountered many hurting and suffering Christians who have retreated into a 'cave' of silence, too afraid to speak about their struggle because they sense that others may see them as a whingeing burden. I feel like God has stuck a radar on my head and is making me aware of those who struggle, so that I can **really** ask them the question, "How are you?"

I let them know that I am genuinely interested, and that I don't want them to just respond with the customary, "I am fine, thanks!" I genuinely desire to know how they truly are. I can see how difficult it is for them to speak openly and freely about how they feel, and I can sense that they have most probably been on the receiving end of other people's remarks for their continued suffering.

Today, the question, "Hi! How are you?" has been relegated to a mere pleasantry; a simple greeting which just means, "Hello!" I am not sure why we add those extra words, "How are you?" onto the end of our greeting because it seems to me that no one really has any time to find out how anyone is anymore. This is very sad, especially when it is occurring among those in the Church. According to God's word, in Galatians 6:2, we are exhorted to bear one another's burdens, and by so doing we are fulfilling the law of Christ. Bearing one another's burdens means carrying the load **with** that person; making their load feel lighter, sharing with them in their suffering.

The definition of the term 'bearing a burden' as rendered in thefreedictionary.com is as follows:

*"To endure something distressing, painful, stressful, or emotionally or physically taxing, **especially for the sake of others.**"* (author's emphasis)

So, when we obey God's word to bear one another's burdens, we are helping them to endure whatever their distressing, painful, stressful, or emotionally or physically taxing burden is. The fact that God's word says we are to bear one another's burdens clearly indicates that believers **will** have sufferings that require other believers to come alongside them to help them bear their burden, for however long that may be.

Nowhere in God's word have I been able to find a scripture that says we are not supposed to have any burdens, let alone not be suffering, whether that is in the case of health issues or other kinds of suffering. There seems to be a culture in the Church today that believes that suffering and burdens must be **'prayed away'**, but after 27 years of trying to pray away the suffering of my health issues, I have come to the conclusion that my healing hasn't happened for a reason, which you will discover as you read through this book.

So, in the hope that sharing my life will resonate with many who silently struggle with unrelenting suffering and pain as they follow Christ, I will now open the door on my life and ask if you would put on your walking boots and accompany me as we embark upon the journey down 'Weary Lane'...

My Tummy Hurts!

When I was very young, about 3 years old, I remember having tummy ache a lot. I can remember having to take medication to help me go to the loo. I assumed this was just normal for children. At that young age, I would not have had the understanding to question it. When I was 11-14 years old, I was at boarding school, and I can recall having tummy ache a lot then too. When I started work at the age of 17, each day I was plagued with endless trips to the loo, and my department manager asked me why I had so many toilet breaks. It was very embarrassing, as a female, having to explain my problem to a male manager. I told him that I could not help needing to rush to the loo.

I had tests done at the hospital, investigating for Crohn's Disease, Ulcerative Colitis and other sorts of bowel conditions. Nothing was diagnosed, and so they labelled it as Irritable Bowel Syndrome. Armed with medication to supposedly ease the symptoms, I tried as best I could to get on with my life.

Each day was a constant battle. I never knew what my tummy was going to be like, or what level of pain I was going to be in. I spent my working days sitting in my office chair in agony, but somehow having to function as if I was fine. I longed for my lunch break just so that I could escape the office and sit on a bench in a park to relax for an hour. The pain would still be there, but at least I was able to momentarily escape the stresses of work which only made my tummy more painful. I longed to get home and crawl into bed with hot water bottles on my tummy. This was my daily life at work, for thirteen years.

The Breakdown

During this time, I also suffered an emotional and physical breakdown, and was referred to a psychiatric hospital for assessment. I was terrified they would 'cart me off' in a straight-jacket, so I ran out of the clinic and screamed out to God to help me. I believed that God existed, but I had no relationship with Him. I didn't read the Bible and I didn't go to church. But somehow, deep down, I knew God was the only One who could help me; and so, unknowingly, I began my search for God. This part of the story will continue in Chapter 2.

After that experience at the psychiatric hospital, my doctor made me feel like a hopeless case, struck me off her list and called me a time-waster, which left me feeling suicidal because I had no one to turn to for help. But still I struggled on with my daily life, with unrelenting pain in my tummy. The breakdown left me with Agoraphobia and Claustrophobia at the same time. When I was indoors, I was desperate to get outside, but when I was outside, I got so panicky that I became desperate to get back indoors. It was a horrendous nightmare. Added to this, I began to develop OCD (Obsessive Compulsive Disorder) habits, but thankfully fairly mildly. A new doctor put me on tranquilisers, antidepressants and sleeping pills all at the same time. I was like a zombie. I soon became addicted to the medication, but somehow, I managed to wean myself off them all after a few months.

Desperate for Healing

Still not knowing Christ at that time, I was so desperate to find a measure of healing that I then ventured into trying to heal myself through the practices of New Age healers. I got involved in these practices out of sheer desperation and ignorance. When you are at rock bottom, and you are not a follower of Christ, you seek help in all the wrong places. I did not know that receiving these New Age healing practices would open me up to being oppressed by 'unholy spirits' which would further affect my life and my health.

I will leave that subject right there because, now being a follower of Christ, I know that what I ventured into was the kingdom of darkness, which I have since confessed and repented of, and have cut off all influence that it will have had on my life at that time.

A Baby Girl...plus More Ailments

Despite being chronically unwell - physically, emotionally and spiritually - in 1990 I became pregnant, but my pregnancy was fraught with difficulties and I had to stop work when I was six months pregnant. After my daughter was born in 1991, I was so ill from blood loss that I was critically anaemic. I stayed in the hospital for five days, and then they discharged me, but as I was on my way out of the hospital, a nurse came up to me and told me that I was supposed to have had two blood transfusions, but somehow the hospital 'forgot'! She said that I could go home and take medication and eat foods containing high levels of iron to help raise my iron level instead of having the blood transfusions, so that's what I did.

However, the medication aggravated my tummy troubles, so I had to stop taking it. This left me with very low iron levels, as the iron in the foods was not sufficient enough to increase it. I lived my life as a new mother in a complete daze of exhaustion, brain fog, and pain. My weight plummeted to around seven stones, when it should have been around nine stones. I was very jaundiced from the lack of iron.

My life was like this for so long that it was one big blur. I somehow managed to function each day out of sheer determination, for the sake of my child, but the overriding memory I have is that it was one long journey of nonstop pain.

Now What's Going On?

At the age of only 39, I began to have menopausal symptoms. What a shock that was at such an early age! My doctor agreed that I was having the menopause early, but that he could not do anything about it until I reached the age of 45, as that was their minimum age to begin treatment, and that I was not to come and discuss it again until then. Yes, you read that correctly! I was shocked by this, and I did not know what to do. I was not computer literate at that time, and was not able to find out what type of self-help was available, so I felt dismissed once again as a time waster.

When I reached 45, I was then called in for tests and they discovered that I had early onset Osteopenia. Well surprise, surprise! Is it any wonder that came on early too, since I had already had six years of menopausal symptoms, without any kind of treatment to prevent its onset?! However, the doctor told me that I didn't need any medication for the Osteopenia either! This seemed odd to me, but I hesitantly accepted his opinion on this. A few years later, I was then called in for a bone-density scan and was told by the consultant that the Osteopenia had now advanced to Osteoporosis and Arthritis! I was 55 years old. As a general rule, most women do not even begin having menopausal symptoms until they are about 55, let alone have Osteoporosis and Arthritis at that age! This time, I was given medication, but my body reacted severely to it and so, once again, it left me with nothing to help alleviate my suffering.

During all of this, my body began to ache deeply. I found that I struggled to hold myself up straight. My muscles hurt all over my body. It took about five years for my doctor to agree that I probably had Fibromyalgia. The exhaustion of just getting myself up and functioning each day whilst in so much pain for over twenty years has resulted in the 'blanket' diagnosis of Chronic Fatigue Syndrome.

EMF Sensitivity? – What is that?

Added to the above, I now also seem to be affected by EMF sensitivity; that is the electromagnetic frequency that emits from all our electrical gadgets, e.g. mobile phones, computers, the TV etc. I have to limit my time on these things, and when I start to feel an acute loss of energy very suddenly, together with an inability to focus or concentrate on anything, then I know that I have EMF build-up in my body. I have to go outside and stand on the ground with bare feet for a while in order to discharge the build-up in my body. This is known as 'earthing' and is simply taking off your shoes and socks and walking around on the earth with bare feet, like you do when you are on the beach. It is called 'earthing', as the principle is the same as that of electrical appliances being earthed so that we don't electrocute ourselves on them. The site I used for this is www. earthing.com which will explain what earthing is.

Some readers may think this is a strange or unconventional way to treat an ailment. But I know that this effect is real because when I am feeling well enough to go to the beach for an afternoon, (which is thankfully only half a mile away from our home!), within ten minutes of walking around on the sand with bare feet, all of the aches, pains and weariness subside, and my energy begins to return. The longer I am out in the natural environment the better it is for my body. When I then go back home, within ten minutes of being indoors, I can feel all of my symptoms returning. It is not a figment of my imagination, because if I go outside and stand on the grass, the symptoms subside again.

Anything Else?

I have limped along through life, struggling with one thing on top of another. With only the customary ten-minute appointments at the doctor's surgery, I have felt unheard and dismissed by those I hoped would help me. My experience of the general practice of the health service seems to be that of giving patients a quick-fix treatment for their outward symptoms. Some simple ailments can be healed this way, but in more complex and chronic cases, many patients don't respond to this approach to health care.

Many people have a multitude of symptoms that stem from just one root cause, yet with so much pressure, lack of funding and under-resourcing in the medical profession, it seems they do not have the time to dig deeper to discover what those root causes are. If the underlying cause of a sufferer's ailments was diagnosed and then eliminated, it is likely that the body would begin to heal naturally, as God created it to do. But if no one has the time to find the cause, many are left with a whole host of physical symptoms that affect their life on a daily, monthly and yearly basis.

More recently, I had a variety of blood tests done for the Chronic Fatigue Syndrome, and one of the results showed a raise in the level of Bilirubin. When it is raised even by just a few points, it becomes known as Gilbert's Syndrome. It is too complicated for me to describe, but in simple terms it is something that affects the liver function, causing fatigue, jaundice, digestive problems and abdominal pain, brain fog, muscle fatigue and muscle pain, and a host of other things. I read an article on a self-help website (www.gilbertssyndrome.org.uk) that suggested a possible connection of Gilbert's Syndrome and menopausal symptoms. If this is the case, then early menopause at the age of 39 would suggest the early onset of Osteoporosis, both from which I suffer. (All of these sound rather familiar!)

My test results also showed my iron level is still very low, in the category of Iron Deficiency Anaemia, and there is even an indicator on the results that my kidney function is at a level which could suggest that of stage-two kidney disease. I found all this out for **myself** by scouring the details of my online medical records. What concerns me is that no doctor has told me any of this, except for one doctor who told me about the Gilbert's Syndrome. But even then, he told me to 'not think about it' because there was nothing that the medical profession could do about it! Needless-to-say, I have done my own research on it, so that I can take measures to help myself.

Coping with Everyday

The overriding thing that plagues my life is the exhaustion, muscle pain and the limiting unpredictability of IBS. Each day it takes about five hours for my body to get to a place where it is able to function on some sort of 'coping' level. Even just having a shower and getting dressed results in so much weariness that I have to get back into bed for about an hour to recover from the effort involved. Needless-to-say, since coming to Christ in 1992 (which I share in Chapter 2), getting to church for 10am has been impossible for me to do. I am only able to get to evening meetings because by that time the weariness has lifted enough to be able to go out. My best hours are between 2pm and 9pm. I still ache all over, but the weariness is less intense during those hours.

But the mornings are really difficult for me, from the time I wake up until about 1pm. Gradually after that, things begin to improve. By the time I go to bed, I feel relatively okay. But when I wake up each morning, it is as if I have been run over by a truck during the night! I am as stiff as a board, every muscle aches, and pain radiates throughout my whole body. Day in and day out, this is my life, which no one but my husband sees, and he is the only one who truly understands just what goes on each day for me.

He is **very** protective of my need for silence, solitude and a daily routine that prevents intrusion into my life, especially in the mornings. We cannot have people to stay over because of the enormous stress that this causes my body, and we cannot stay with others either, for the same reason. When we go on holiday, we don't travel until the afternoon when I feel slightly more 'with it', and we have to book self-catering cottages where we can have our own privacy and where I can maintain my routine. We used to stay in guest houses or hotels, but as the years have gone on and my physical ailments seem to be wearing me down even more, I can no longer do that because the owners usually require guests to vacate their rooms by about 10 am so that they can clean them.

Living with all these things is very wearying and restrictive, and when people see me at an evening church meeting and ask me why they don't see me at the morning services, I find myself wearily trying to explain to them the reasons why. Usually, their well-intentioned response to my explanation is, "Have you had prayer for this?" After spending over a quarter of a century praying to God on my own, and with others, for healing of all of these things, I am sure you can imagine what I would like to say in response…but thankfully the Holy Spirit restrains me.

This is the snapshot of my walk down 'Weary Lane'. I could add more, but this is enough to give you the general idea of what my everyday life is like.

Chapter 2

Seek and you shall Find

"So I say to you, ask and keep on asking, and it will be given to you; seek and keep on seeking, and you will find; knock and keep on knocking, and the door will be opened to you. For everyone who keeps on asking [persistently], receives; and he who keeps on seeking [persistently], finds; and to him who keeps on knocking [persistently], the door will be opened."
Luke 11:9-10 AMP

In this chapter I would like to share with you my testimony of the lengths that God will go to, to reach down and save a lost sinner. I will then share with you what has happened since I became a believer. This will build on the picture of what I wrote in Chapter 1, and the story will conclude later, in Chapter 6 – *When Healing Doesn't Happen – God's Purpose in the Pain.*

My Dad was a Royal Navy Officer, and in the early 1970's, our family was relocated from the UK to Gibraltar. I was ten years old. So that we could integrate into life there, I joined the Gibraltar Cathedral Choir, along with my two sisters. When I was thirteen, whilst at a Church of England boarding school in the UK, I was confirmed by the Bishop of Portsmouth. Joining the choir and being confirmed were more of a 'nice thing to do' rather than a conscious decision to give my life to Christ and follow Him, but I guess that a seed must have been sown in my heart, which would lay dormant for many years… and be awakened much further on in my life.

In 1979, I was given a Bible for my eighteenth birthday. I kept that Bible in pristine condition for many years, but never picked it up to read.

I mentioned in Chapter 1 that, before I came to Christ in 1992, my life was a mess, both physically and spiritually, having been involved in New Age practices in the vain hope of finding some level of healing for my long-term health conditions. I was also enslaved in the ways and the sins of the world in the hope of finding love, happiness and security. I was as low as I could possibly be. I felt so worthless, unnoticed, and insignificant…like a speck of dust that could be blown away by a gust of wind at any moment.

The Search Begins

I started going to a church in the autumn of 1990, but I was just going there because I did not know what else to do. I felt a measure of stability each Sunday, but I did not know that I could actually know God for real through having faith in Jesus Christ to save me, because no one ever preached about it. It was one of those churches where everything was done by rote, everyone was comfortable in their pews, the sermons were pleasant but powerless, and the presence of the Lord was nowhere to be seen. Despite this, I kept going, mainly for the sake of my new baby, who arrived in May 1991. Even though I did not know Christ, I wanted to bring my daughter up in some sort of church environment.

During this time, from my pregnancy in 1990 to the time my daughter was 1 year old in May 1992, God must have seen into my heart and known that I needed to find Him, even though I was in a church that did not seem to think that it was necessary to tell its congregation what they must do to be saved. God can see a searching heart, and He will do whatever it takes to make sure that we find Him.

God Invades My Life

It was at the Good Friday service in 1992, that God decided it was time to invade my life.

At this service, they had erected a huge wooden cross at the front of the church. At some point in the service we began singing the old hymn, 'When I Survey the Wondrous Cross'. As I was singing, I started to sob silently but very deeply, and I also began to shake. I did not know what was happening to me. I decided to look at the huge wooden cross again, hoping that it might give me some sort of answer to my sobbing and shaking, when, all of a sudden, I heard a very powerful voice saying to me, "There is more; seek and you shall find."

As someone who did not know much about the Christian faith, let alone read the Bible, when I heard this voice speak these words, it felt like an arrow had pierced my soul. I was so startled by this that I thought I must be imagining it! I looked around me to see if anyone else in the church had heard it and possibly showing any signs of distress, but everyone looked their usual comfortable selves. By this time my sobbing and shaking were getting so intense that the people in the pews around me were looking uncomfortable at my display of 'abnormal' church behaviour! So, I sat down and somehow managed to compose myself.

It then dawned upon me that I must have had an encounter with God, and that He had spoken directly to me, in response to the desperate cries of my soul over the previous years. His words to me felt like a holy command to seek and find whatever it was He wanted me to find. His word was, "There is more". More than what, I asked myself? I had heard those words as I was staring at the wooden cross. It was the day that the Church reflects upon Jesus' crucifixion on the cross, so God must have been saying to me that there was something beyond Jesus' crucifixion that He wanted me to find. I didn't have a clue what it was, but I knew that if God Himself was going to take the trouble to invade my life in such a way and speak to me personally, then I had better obey Him, and I was determined to seek and find whatever was missing in the preaching of this church I was attending.

Even though I had been going to this church for eighteen months, the reality hit me that I did not know Christ at all. The extent of my knowledge and understanding of Christianity was that both God and Jesus existed, that Jesus had been crucified on a cross, had died and risen to life again, and had ascended into heaven. But what I didn't know was that there was a purpose for it all.

Having had that encounter, and hearing God speak directly to me, I went home and decided that it was time to be courageous and to talk to God myself, and ask Him to reveal to me the missing part of the puzzle; the thing that was needed and was essential in order for me to go from a life of sitting on a pew to a life that was truly that of a follower of Christ. This was so important to me that it really was a pivotal moment in my life. I knew that I could not move forward in life until I had **found** and **received** what God wanted me to **know** and to **have**.

There is More; Seek and you shall Find

Within a few days of this experience, I came across a group of Christians doing an outreach in the town where I lived, and I was intrigued to find out what their message was about. I felt the Lord was prompting me to do this, because I was a frightened, messed up young woman, and no way would I have voluntarily gone up to a bunch of total strangers in the street!

As soon as they spoke to me, I knew that what they were saying **had** to be the missing piece of the puzzle. They showed me in the Bible, in John Chapter 3, that Jesus said we must be born again of water and of the Spirit in order to enter the kingdom of heaven. These Christians then showed me in the Bible that after Jesus ascended into heaven, a further event occurred on the Day of Pentecost, where Jesus poured out the Holy Spirit upon all the disciples who were gathered together, and they all began to speak in tongues (in languages that they had never learned). This really caught my attention!

I had heard the words 'Holy Spirit' mentioned in some services, but I had no idea what the minister was talking about, and no one ever explained what the Holy Spirit was, let alone tell us that we needed to be born again and filled with the Holy Spirit, which would bestow us with the accompanying gift of speaking in tongues (read the whole of Acts Chapter 2, and what Jesus said in Mark 16:9-20).

These Christians also showed me in Acts 2:38-39, that this gift of the Holy Spirit was a promise from God to **all** who would believe in His Son Jesus Christ, not just for those first believers. I was stunned by what I was being shown in the Bible! No one had ever preached this to me before, and I was shocked at the realisation that many mainstream churches are failing to do this.

Millions of people who go to church, week after week, year after year, are not getting saved because no one is telling them what **Jesus Himself said** they must do to be saved. I was one such person, christened as a baby, confirmed at thirteen, going to church for 18 months, singing the hymns and even taking communion, but I **was not** saved! What a huge shock that was…

Filled with the Holy Spirit

I felt the Lord convicting me with the truth of His word, and I knew that I needed to ask the Lord to save me and fill me with His Holy Spirit because I deeply hungered and thirst for a truly biblical relationship with God; the same as those first believers. These Christians invited me to a social event the following evening, which I decided I would go to, but before that, I went home and picked up the Bible that had been given to me in 1979. I scoured all the passages of scripture that these Christians had shown me so that I could read them for myself. I was completely stunned at what was jumping off the pages at me, and I began to treasure that Bible.

I went to the social event the following evening, and a group of these Christians guided me through a prayer asking the Lord to save me, and to fill me with the Holy Spirit. Having never done this sort of thing before, I didn't know what to do other than to just start saying the Lord's Prayer, and also to say the word 'Hallelujah', which means 'praise the Lord', so I felt that this was an appropriate word to keep saying.

Within a few minutes I began to speak words that were not English! I hesitated at first, a bit frightened at speaking words that I did not recognise or understand. But I decided to surrender to God, and began saying 'Hallelujah' again, and immediately words of a different language came pouring out of my mouth like an unstoppable river! I knew that God had filled me with the Holy Spirit! Praise the Lord! When I got home that night, I was a bit anxious that this may have all been a strange dream, and so I decided to go into each room of the house and get on my knees and pray. As I said the word 'Hallelujah' again, immediately it changed into an unknown tongue! I then went out into the garden at midnight, and sat under a tree, and began to pray again, and the same thing happened! I was jumping for joy all around the garden, in the dark!

Baptised by Full Immersion

I can't really remember whether I slept much that night because of the joy that was overflowing in my heart! The next day, I went to their afternoon church service for the very first time, where I heard the pastor preach about baptism by full immersion in water. This was something that I had **never** heard before either, but it was right there in the Bible, where 3,000 were baptised in the Jordan river on the Day of Pentecost!

I had read in one of the church's pamphlets that they had a baptism pool which they filled up every Sunday, ready for anyone who wanted to get baptised. The pastor showed from the Bible that in the New Testament, those who believed the Gospel and became followers of Christ got baptised by full immersion immediately. There was no delay, no baptism course to attend before the event. I was stunned at how simple it all was, and I wondered why this simplicity was being kept secret by the mainstream churches, yet here was this non-denominational church that seemed to fully understand the simplicity of obeying the word of God.

I felt the Lord urging me not to debate or hesitate over this, but to simply obey His word to be baptised. The pastor read the scriptures out that even Jesus was baptised in the Jordan river, by John the Baptist! So, who was I to argue with God over something that even His Son obeyed?!

So, I got baptised that very day, in 1992, at the age of thirty. In fact, I was so eager to obey God's word and get baptised, after having been filled with the Holy Spirit the night before, that I had packed a change of clothes and brought them with me, to put on for the baptism!

At that moment, I then realised that, without a doubt, the words that I heard the Lord speak to me at the Good Friday service in my previous church – "There is more; seek and you shall find" – were being fulfilled right there and then. He promised that if I sought, then I would find. I had not known anything about baptism by full immersion, nor did I know anything about the baptism of the Holy Spirit, but God made sure that I found the truth in the Bible, and then convicted me to obey His instructions.

On Fire for God!

My Bible became my constant companion, and I devoured the word of God for hours each day. I was on fire for the Lord for two years, telling people about God, about sin, about salvation and everything I could possibly tell them from God's word. God had transformed my life of despair into a life of joy and hope, and I wanted to tell people about it. Most people said "Oh, that's nice for you!", but they personally seemed unaffected by what I was saying to them. This concerned me immensely. I could not work out why they would not want to receive this amazing salvation for themselves.

During this two-year period, I prayed for people to be healed, and God answered these prayers. I prayed for healings for myself, and God healed these as well, (I will share some stories of these healings in the next chapter). However, I was still left with all the conditions that I had before I came to Christ. For some reason these did not get healed. This baffled me, but I tried not to let it send me into despair again.

What is Happening, Lord?

But to continue my story, in 1994 certain life events and circumstances caused me to become weary again, and my faith started to weaken. I began to slide back into my previous sinful lifestyle, and I made some big mistakes repeatedly. I felt like I was in the grip of something that was enticing me and trapping me in a vicious cycle of sinful behaviour. What shocked me was that no one at this new church had warned me early on in my faith that falling back into sin was actually possible to do, **as a believer!** I had thought that once I had given my life to Christ and had been baptised and filled with the Holy Spirit, then my life would never revert to my old sinful ways. What a shock it was to discover that sin was crouching at my door, waiting to pounce on me again.

This left me very confused and even frightened. I struggled with how I could proclaim that I was a follower of Christ, yet at the same time be caught up again in the sinful behaviour of my past.

Go, and Sin No More

Having been in this church for two years, I knew very well the story in the Bible of the woman caught in adultery. In John Chapter 8 verses 10-11, after Jesus had said to her accusers, *"Let he among you that is without sin cast the first stone at her",* Jesus then said to the woman, *"Go, and **sin no more**."* NKJV (author's emphasis)

The New International Version translation puts it this way:

*"Go now, and **leave your life of sin**."* (author's emphasis)

These are **Jesus' own words**, and they apply to **all** who have given their lives to Him. But I had failed to obey Jesus' command to *"Go, and sin no more"*. I did go, but I sinned again and again, falling back into the sins I used to be involved in.

Despite the turmoil I was in, I clung to the Lord as my only hope. I wanted to be free from the torment of these repetitive sinful behaviours, but I felt powerless to stop them, even though I regularly prayed and fasted, and commanded these demons to flee in Jesus' name.

This went on for **seventeen years…**

The Wilderness of Isolation

With the lack of help from this church (that had shown me what I needed to do to be saved) I eventually stopped going in 1999. It was a deeply distressing period in my life as a believer, and I began to fellowship with the Lord on my own, every single day, in my own home. I would put on worship CDs and sing my soul out to Him. I immersed myself in the Bible for hours each day, and I prayed for at least an hour a day.

During these times, the health problems that I had before I came to Christ still plagued me, and this caused me to seek Him even harder. In my times of isolation, when I prayed, I found that the Lord would speak things to me, just like He did at the Good Friday service in 1992. I began to write down all the things He spoke to me. His words sustained me through the many years of isolation I had to endure.

I will leave this part of the story at this point, but I will pick it up again in Chapter 6.

Healings that Happen…When others Don't Happen

But now, I would like you to journey with me into the next chapter, where I share with you the wonderful stories of healings that have occurred during my life in Christ, to demonstrate to you that just because some healings do not happen in our own lives, God still uses us to pray for others to be healed, and that God does heal them even though **we personally** may still not be healed of the things that plague us.

The subject of our not being healed, even though we are demonstrating the evidence of faith by others being healed when we pray for them, is a troubling mystery, and I will discuss this in more depth in Chapter 6. But for now, I will just say that when something is happening in our life and is a mystery to us, it takes us into the realm of walking the path of faith, day in and day out, with no glimmer of any change on the horizon. At times it can be gruelling, but God is able to use our time of suffering for His purpose and for His glory. . . as you will see as you continue to read this book.

Chapter 3

Healings that have Happened!

Let me begin this chapter by stating that I very much believe in prayer for healing, and that I believe that God can and does heal. I have never doubted this, not even one tiny bit, which you will see as I share with you the accounts of some real-life healings that God has given to me for myself, (although not for the things that continue to trouble me on a daily basis), and also for others who I have prayed for in Jesus' name. This is to give glory to God, and for which I take no credit whatsoever. When God has used me to pray for people to be healed, I have simply been the vessel that He has used to offer prayer to them so that He could manifest a miraculous healing.

So, let's begin the exciting adventure of seeing the wonderful healings that **have** happened!

My Daughter

My daughter has had many healings, but I will share just two with you here, as they involve me hearing the voice of God in both situations, where I then had to obey and act immediately on what I heard.

Eczema

My daughter had eczema on her fingers from a very young age.

They were very dry and scaly, and I used to just apply lotion to help keep them moisturized. Then one day, when she was about nine years old, I noticed that her finger nails were going yellow and turning up at the edges! They looked unsightly, and I was rather concerned. I prayed about this but didn't seem to get any answer, at first.

My daughter drank milk each day, so I felt that the nail problem could not be related to any calcium deficiency. This problem went on for a month or so, and her nails were getting worse. I was at the point of taking her to see the doctor but decided to call on the Lord with a great fervency. I sat in a chair and shouted very loudly to God, "Please tell me what to do Lord because I am at my wits end! I am not going to move until you tell me what to do!"

As I sat there, silently, after yelling out to God, all of a sudden, I heard a voice as loud as thunder, shouting out of the heavens. Rather surprisingly, the word I heard was, "MILK"! Without **any** questioning, I leapt up off the chair, immediately ran to the kitchen and poured loads of milk into a bottle, then went to collect my daughter from school. When she got in the car, I told her what had happened, and literally ordered her to drink the entire bottle of milk! Three times each day she drank a large glass of milk, and each day her eczema and her nails began to improve. After a week her eczema had vanished and her yellow and turned up nails had completely healed!

Strange Spots

When my daughter was about eleven years old, she started to get some strange-looking lumpy spots on the inside of one of her legs. They looked like purple chicken-pox spots. At first, I thought they would just disappear after a week or so, but they started to increase in number. I didn't like the look of them at all, so I took her to the medical centre. The doctor took one look at them and, with a rather puzzled look on her face, she just said "Umm"! Somewhat concerned by her response, I asked her what the problem was. She said, "I have read about such spots in medical journals but have never ever come across a case of them in the whole of my medical career! Your daughter has a case of a viral skin disease, there is no treatment for it, and it is likely to spread further."

I was absolutely flabbergasted at this news. How could my lovely young daughter have developed an untreatable skin disease? It reminded me of stories in the Bible, where people had a skin disease known as leprosy, and to my rather anxious maternal ears, it sounded to me like the doctor had just told me that my daughter had a form of leprosy! She showed us some photos of the condition in her medical book, and tried to reassure us that it would eventually clear up, but may take two years to do so.

We went home and somehow got on with every day life, but inside I felt numb. I kept praying for the lumps to be healed but they only got worse, and they spread even more, just as the doctor had said. I tried to put it out of my mind, but it was difficult because it affected my daughter, and I am sure every parent who is reading this will know just how all-consuming it is when something horrible comes against your child, and you feel powerless to make it all better for them.

A few months went by, and we decided to go away on holiday to the seaside. On one lovely hot and sunny day, my daughter decided to walk down to the sea to have a paddle. I was silently sitting up on the beach, watching her splash her feet in the sea. Whilst I was looking at her thoughtfully, and thinking about her lumps which were visible when she was in her swimwear, the sound of a mighty voice pierced my silence, and it startled me so much that my heart began to race. The voice said just one word, and it was the **only** word that I needed to hear to catapult me into action!

The word was, '**Naaman**'!

I knew the biblical story of the man named Naaman. He had leprosy; a skin disease. He was told to go to the Jordan river and wash his skin seven times. After he had obeyed Elisha's instructions, his skin disease was completely healed! (see 2 Kings Chapter 5).

Hearing that one word, 'Naaman', was enough to cause me to jump up off the sand and run down to the sea as fast as I could! I knew **exactly** what God was telling me to do. He wanted me to wash my daughter's skin disease seven times with the sea water. I hurriedly explained all this to my daughter and asked her to believe that God was about to heal her of this awful condition.

I bent down and scooped up big handfuls of seawater and splashed it all over her lumps, seven times, whilst praying to God to heal them, and giving Him thanks for breaking through into this situation by giving me His answer.

After that, we just trusted God that He would fulfil His word. The next morning, I boldly asked my daughter to let me see her legs. The 'leprous' lumps had completely shrivelled up, and all that remained was the scar tissue, like you get after chicken-pox spots have faded! We were absolutely ecstatic, and jumped around the room, giving glory to God! The scars remained for many years almost like a sign from God to remind us of what an awesome healing miracle He did that day. But my daughter has recently told me that they have now completely healed, with no visible marks at all! Glory be to God!

My Sister

When my sister, Sharon, first came to the Lord, she was staying at my home for a while. I brought a boiling hot mug of tea to her, and somehow, the entire mug spilled out onto her legs. She screamed in agony as the boiling tea scolded her skin. Both of us immediately began to pray to God in the Spirit, in tongues. In the natural, she should have had burn marks on her legs, but whilst we were praying, the agonising burning subsided, and no scold marks or blistering occurred. Glory be to God!

A Friend

Many years ago, a neighbour, who knew that I was a Christian, rang me up to say that she was in agony, and had been flat on her back for three days with a slipped disc. She said to me, "I had to ring you because I know that you are the only one who can help me, because you believe in God and because you pray." I responded by telling her that I personally could not help her, but I would pray to the One who could help her. It was a Sunday. The church I went to at that time thankfully had afternoon meetings, so I was able to get to the services. I told my neighbour that I would put her prayer request to the pastor to announce it to the whole congregation so that we would all be praying for her at about 4pm.

I then told her the Bible story of the man who was begging for money at the temple gates, who had been unable to walk since birth, and how Peter and John looked at him and told him that they didn't have any money to give him, but had something better than money to give to him. Then I quoted the following scripture to her of what Peter said to the lame man, and I told her that at about 4pm she was to know that we were praying for her, and to believe this passage.

"Then Peter said, "Silver and gold I do not have, but what I do have I give you: In the name of Jesus Christ of Nazareth, rise up and walk." – Acts 3:6 NKJV

After I had finished talking to her, I went to church, told the pastor of her need for prayer, and at 4pm the whole congregation prayed for God to heal her.

The following day the phone rang. It was my neighbour. She struggled to speak through emotion but managed to say to me that at 4pm, whilst she was still in agony on her bed, she heard a loud snapping noise and felt something happening in her spine. She then got up off her bed and walked and jumped around in joy! Glory be to God!

See John 4:43-54 for a biblical account of another 'same-hour' miracle.

A Neighbour's Daughter

Also, at that time, another neighbour of mine had a daughter who had been sick for three weeks. The doctors could not work out what was causing it, and she wasn't getting any better. My neighbour, who lived next door to us, knew we were Christians as we had weekly house groups at our home, and they could hear us singing in our times of worship. Whilst my neighbour was telling me about her daughter's illness, I asked her if she would like us to pray for her to be healed. She looked a bit uncomfortable about it but said that she would 'try anything once'!

During our house meeting that same evening, I told everyone about what I had said to my neighbour, and as a group, we asked God to heal her child.

The next afternoon, I looked out of the window and saw my neighbour pull up on her driveway. I then saw her daughter jump out of the car in her school uniform! I ran out of my front door in excitement and went up to the little girl and told her how wonderful it was that she was now better, and that we had prayed for her that God would heal her. She gave me a big smile. I then went up to my neighbour and said the same thing, and I assured her that we had prayed for her daughter in our house group the previous evening. My neighbour looked really uncomfortable, as though she didn't know what to do with the fact that God had healed her child. She grabbed her daughter and made a hasty retreat into her house. Shortly after this, they moved out of the neighbourhood and I haven't seen them since.

This is a sad example of the reaction of someone who has an encounter with God, but doesn't know what to do with it. I continue to pray for them that God will draw them to Him so that they can be saved.

My Husband

I am typing this story the very morning after my husband has received a miracle healing! He went to bed at 5pm yesterday afternoon (20th February 2019) because he felt a bit weary and wanted to have a rest before dinner. So, I left him to it whilst I prepared the meal. At 6pm, I called up to him to come down for dinner, but I heard a deep groaning noise and raced up the stairs to see what was happening.

He whispered a few disjointed words saying that he was feeling ghastly, with an intense pain in his head that was making him restless, agitated, nauseous and unable to communicate. He looked very pale and distressed. My husband is rarely unwell. If he gets a cold or cough, he just soldiers on with work. It has to be something really awful to make him need to crawl into bed. He didn't want me to call the doctor, so I immediately prayed the most basic and simple prayer to the Lord, saying, "Dear God, please heal Chris… please heal Chris. Thank you Lord. Amen".

I left the room and went down to eat my dinner alone, but with the prayer going constantly round in my head. I went up to check on him an hour later and he was asleep. I checked again at 9pm and he was still asleep. I slept in a separate room so as not to disturb him.

The next morning, I heard him get up and go downstairs to put the kettle on. When I got downstairs, he was all happy and smiling, and said to me, "You have got your happy husband back!" He said he felt really well and full of energy. I asked him when he started to feel better, and he said to me, "Immediately after you prayed for me"! Praise be to God!

Myself

I would like to share the stories of some miraculous healings that the Lord has given to me, even whilst my life-long ailments have remained.

Foot Injury

One morning I got up and went downstairs to put the kettle on. When I got to the last two steps on the stairs, somehow, I slipped off and as my left foot hit the floor, I heard a very loud snapping noise. My foot had turned inwards, and I could not move it to straighten it out again. Two of my toes had also 'dropped' and were pointing downwards instead of being up straight next to the others. I was screaming in pain, and I knew that it must be a serious injury. Through gritted teeth I called out to God to help me, whilst I prayed in tongues through great sobs of pain.

As I was praying, I then saw my toes rise back up to their normal position! I was stunned at this and gave praise to God. We went to the hospital to get my foot checked out because it was still turned inwards. I told them about the toes that had dropped but were now back to normal. They did an x-ray and found tissue damage to the tendons that attached to those two toes, but that the tissue had 'restored itself'! (God healed it!). The rest of my foot was suffering from this tendon trauma and they said that as it slowly healed, it would swell right up but would straighten itself back to the normal position eventually. They told me that I would need to use crutches for three weeks, and that I was not to put a shoe on that foot or to put any weight on my foot for two weeks.

I went home with the crutches and when I got indoors, I prayed, asking God to heal my foot **so fast** that I would be able put shoes on and walk without the crutches in three days, **not** three weeks. On day three, I got up and got dressed and put my shoes on and walked my daughter to school normally! Praise the Lord!

Cut Finger

One day I was preparing dinner and I deeply cut my finger. Blood was pouring out and I could not stem the flow. I called out to God to help me, and began praying fervently in tongues for several minutes, and I asked God to close the wound miraculously. As I looked at my finger, I saw the cut heal over right in front of my eyes! Praise and glory be to God!

Oven Spray Injury

Another time, I was cleaning someone's oven whilst they were at work. I was using a very caustic oven spray that rapidly removes burnt-on grease. As I was spraying this product onto the oven, a gust of wind blew through an open window and the oven spray blew onto my face and into one of my eyes. Immediately my face and my eye began to sting and burn. I ran up to the bathroom and began splashing cold water onto my face and into my eye. I saw a blister forming on the surface of my eyeball and my vision began to get blurry. Areas of my face began to get red where the spray was burning the skin. I was praying like crazy for God to help me and heal me, especially my eye, as this was really serious. There was no one else in the house to help me; it was just me and God.

I prayed like this for about ten minutes, constantly checking my face and my eye in the mirror. I then felt all the burning subside, and when I again looked in the mirror, the red patches had gone on my skin and the blister on my eyeball had completely vanished! I began dancing around the house and singing praises to God at the top of my voice!

Shoulder Injury

One evening in December 2013, we had just returned home from shopping. It was dark and wet outside, but I had walked up and down our footpath many times over the three months we had lived there, so I wasn't concerned about it. But this time, my feet slipped from under me and I crashed to the ground, sideways onto my left shoulder. I could not move to get myself up. The pain was unbearable, and I yelled for help. At that moment, my daughter came out of the house to get some more shopping from the car and found me in a heap on the ground. Somehow, she got me up and helped me indoors.

I tried to move my arm up and down and backwards and forwards, but it would not move more than about six inches in any direction. I also had pain in my left ribs. We rushed to the hospital, and they examined me and diagnosed full rotator cuff injury, and some fractured ribs.

Days went into weeks with the pain constantly there, with my arm being unable to move more than the six inches, despite me trying to do some gentle shoulder exercises recommended by my doctor.

I had been praying all this time for God to heal it, but my healing didn't seem to want to happen.

In February 2014, eight weeks after the injury, we heard that a new monthly Christian meeting was starting up in a town near to where we lived. It was an evening meeting, so we decided to go to their first event. I love to lift my arms up in worship but could only lift up my right arm. After the meeting had finished, they had a time of prayer where people could find a quiet corner and pray with members of the ministry team. I decided to go up for prayer. I explained what had happened to me and so the lady prayed for me. She is the lovely kind, who **doesn't** feel the need to test your faith as to whether you have been healed by asking you to fling your arm up in the air the moment she has finished praying!

I thanked her for praying for me, and then walked back to my seat to chat to people. I then felt the Lord whisper to me, "Go into a quiet corner, on your own, and lift up your arm". My heart started racing, and I knew that I had to respond to this prompting.

I found a corner where no one was hovering around, and said, "Okay God. Here goes!". My heart was thumping by this point! I moved my arm slowly up to its limited six-inch position, and then prayed to God asking Him to move it beyond this stuck position. In faith, I willed it to move in Jesus' name. I then found that I could move it very slowly upwards so that it was horizontal with the floor! I lowered it again and then decided I would move it out sideways from the side of my body. Again, my arm lifted up to a horizontal position! I then put my arm across my body with my left hand placed on my right shoulder, and lifted my left elbow upwards, whilst still keeping my left hand on my right shoulder. Again, I could lift it up to horizontal! I ran to tell the lady who had prayed for me. All the team were rejoicing and praising God for this healing!

It took several more months until I could raise my arm fully and do circular movements with it, but on that night when God asked me to move my arm after having had prayer, even being able to lift it up 90 degrees was a complete miracle healing for me, having spent the previous two months with only six inches of movement in all directions! Praise God!

This completes the stories of some of the miraculous healings that have happened on my journey with the Lord. I have shared these healing testimonies with you to show you that God used me to pray for healings for others, and for healings of things for my own self, even whilst still struggling with all the conditions and symptoms that have been a part of my life for so long. He did not look at my long-term ailments and see any lack of faith or unbelief in my life that would render me unfit for His use. On the contrary, He used me whilst **still having** these conditions. He looked at my heart and saw in me the faith and belief I have in Him, that He is able to heal.

God uses many people who have long-term conditions to pray for healing for others, even though they themselves still remain physically unhealed. There are high-profile Christians around the world, some who are paralysed and in wheelchairs, who God is using for His purposes, even though they haven't got up out of their wheelchairs and walked. It is sad when people in the Church, who are blessed with good health, feel the need to cast a shadow over these high-profile ministers, silently or not so silently questioning why they have not been healed. I have heard people do this… and my heart aches deeply, wondering why people feel the need to question the person's lack of healing and then come up with what they think is the 'solution' for the person's suffering.

I know someone who is in a wheelchair, who visits those in hospital and ministers to them, even to those who are dying. This person prayed and ministered to my father-in-law in his dying days, and took time to pray with me and my family after the sudden death of my own father in 2015.

Is it right for any of us to inwardly think that Christians who have a disability of any kind, who remain with their condition whilst still ministering to others, are any less of a Christian because they personally haven't been healed of their disability? Just because some people, due to their suffering, can't get to church at the times that have been 'set in stone' for decades, their lack of attendance each Sunday does not make them a lesser Christian.

It is not our place to decide who God is going to heal, what He is going to heal, or when that healing will be. Our job is to keep our ears open and listen out for God's voice calling us into action to fulfil **His** plan, as and when **He** determines. We should not run ahead of God in anything…especially in the area of healing. Although we are believing in God when we are praying for healing for people, we should not make people feel like we are 'spiritually bullying' them to 'try harder' to get their healing. This type of treatment will not work, and I am sure that God is not pleased with the way some people misuse the ministry of healing.

Yes, of course we would like God to do an instant, miraculous healing, and when we pray for this we can hope that He will do it, but we should not assume that He is going to heal a person miraculously the moment we pray for them. When a miraculous healing **does** happen, then it is clearly God's appointed time for the healing to take place. But the Church is full of people who haven't been healed, and we have to face this fact. Rather than ignoring the silent suffering of the folk who are sitting in our pews, we need to ask God to do something in **our own** hearts to change the way we think about those who suffer, so that we can minister to them by helping to bear their burdens.

I believe that many Christians who suffer with long-term conditions have become disheartened, and have left the Church for good, **not** because of God, but because of encounters with some 'name it, claim it' leaders who may have spoken words that have caused them to feel like a failure after receiving prayer for healing, that hasn't actually healed them. This has happened to me several times, followed by the minister swiftly moving along the line to the next person who has come for prayer… probably also hoping for a healing.

God is watching all of this and His heart must grieve at what He sees happening. And so, this aptly leads us to the next chapter, where I will discuss the issue of those who display what could be termed as a 'scoffing' attitude towards believers who remain unhealed, despite an abundance of prayer.

Chapter 4

The Scorn of the Scoffers

"Listen to me, you who know right from wrong, you who cherish my law in your hearts. Do not be afraid of people's scorn, nor fear their insults."
Isaiah 51:7

This chapter is not intended to be a judgment. Its purpose is to help believers see how we could love each other better, particularly when we are suffering. But in order to show how we can improve in this area, I first need to write about how we seem to be going wrong. This very fact means that some of what I write may feel a bit uncomfortable.

Let's begin by having a look at the meaning of the word 'scorn'. An online search of the most popular dictionaries gives some serious meanings for this word, e.g. to mock, make fun of, ridicule, deride, and to treat with disdain or contempt. The general Google definition also includes some less weighty meanings e.g. to dismiss, and to make light of. For the purpose of this chapter, these latter definitions are more on the lines of what many sufferers may experience from others, although there are times when we can encounter the more serious ones.

Whilst I am sure that none of us would want to knowingly do or say anything to others that could be considered as dismissive or making fun of them, unfortunately it is a fact of life that we can easily do and say things that do cause hurt to others. This usually comes from not thinking before we speak, and originates in a lack of self-control; a lack of taming the tongue; of not bringing all our thoughts and actions into captivity to obey Christ (see 2 Corinthians 10:5). Although there aren't any statistics to prove it, I feel as certain as is possible that many in the Church may have been on the receiving end of things that could be considered as scornful.

I am thankful to God for revealing to me, in the situations where I have received words from others that I would have hoped never to hear, that He was teaching me how to forgive. In order to know how to forgive, we have to be taken into situations that require us to forgive. In the natural, that is not an easy thing to do, and we need all of God's almighty power to help us do so. There were many years where I battled with the deadly emotion of unforgiveness, as I wrestled with the reality that fellow Christians were capable of saying hurtful, and scornful things, whether intentionally or unintentionally.

So, what I write here is not based on any bitterness or unforgiveness. It is simply to give an account of what many long-term suffers can often experience from those within the Church, when we should really be receiving the opposite.

Over these years, I have felt that God has been exposing me to these experiences for a reason, and that reason was to get me to the place where I could write this book. I have come to learn that when God wants a job done, it may not be a comfortable thing to go through.

So, over the next few pages, this is where the journey gets a little uncomfortable, but at the end of the chapter, I will offer the firm but necessary word of God as the remedy to the way that we care for and minister to all who suffer.

Did They Really Just Say That?

As I've mentioned already, I have been praying for 27 years for God to heal me of my ongoing conditions. So far, my constant asking, seeking, and knocking at God's door has not brought about what I long for. During this time, I have encountered indifference, insensitivity, having my ailments made fun of, and sometimes disdain from some within the Church.

When people have prayed for me, but my healing hasn't happened, I have noticed how some begin to keep their distance, which has had the effect of making me feel like an outcast. If I have bumped into them in the high street or a supermarket, and they have asked me how I am, and I say that I am still struggling on, often they look at me with an expression of dismay and a heavy sigh, as if I should be getting over my ailments by now. Then they may go into fix-it mode, asking me countless questions about whether it could be "this" or "that" which may be causing my healing to not happen; or they tell me of a miraculous healing that they have heard about of someone with similar issues to what I have, as if trying to snap me out of what they may perceive to be a lack of faith or unbelief; or they will change the subject very quickly.

Each of these experiences has left me feeling even more weary than I was before I bumped into them. It is extremely exhausting answering someone's questions about why you are still suffering. As I mentioned earlier, when anyone asks me how I am, it is easier to just say "I'm fine thanks!" simply to avoid what I call 'the scorn of the scoffers'.

One such experience happened to me about seven years ago. A lady at a church I attended at that time asked me how I was. She knew that I struggled with health issues that prevented me from being able to get to church in the morning. I was there that evening for a service. Believing this person to be genuinely asking me how I was, I decided to tell her. As soon as I started to tell her, she said to me, "Oh for goodness sake Michele, you have always got something wrong with you!" Needless-to-say, I was so shocked at this that I was literally unable to respond. I felt like someone had just punched me. My husband then appeared and saw me looking completely shaken. I told him what had happened, and he whisked me out of the church as fast as possible. I told him that, if this is what Christian love is like, I never wanted to go back to a church ever again.

This account is not an isolated incident. I have had many people say to me, "It is not God's will for you to be unwell or suffer like this" and "You must try harder, pray harder, and press in until you get your healing". Each time they see me, they say things like "Have you got your healing yet?" When I reply, "No, not yet", they look at me as if I couldn't care less whether God healed me or not! If only they could actually see into my heart, and know just how much I **yearn** to be healed and free of these long-term conditions, and how long I have sought the Lord for it. I have had people tell me of healing retreats that I 'ought' to go to; still others have said things like, "I hope you are going to the healing service next month? This might be your 'moment'".

I know all these people are keen to see me healed, and feel that they should inform me of every possible opportunity there is so that I can be healed. But the constant bombardment borders on what I call 'spiritual harassment'. When I have been on the receiving end of people's seemingly well-intentioned comments, I often wonder if they have ever experienced a period of debilitating, long-term suffering; the kind that can cause you to wonder where God is; the kind of suffering that has the potential to test your faith to its limits?

I have found over the years that it is those who suffer and have sought God to be their comfort and strength **in their suffering,** who are truly the ones who are able to give comfort and help to others who suffer (see 2 Corinthians 1:3-5). In contrast, I have found that those who have not had the 'privilege' of experiencing much suffering are often the ones who are quick off the mark with their 'name it, claim it', sometimes coercive prayers, but soon seem to distance themselves from you when you fail to demonstrate signs of being healed.

I use the word 'privilege' in the paragraph above because in the following verse, God's word describes suffering as a privilege:

*"For you have been given not only the privilege of trusting in Christ but also the **privilege of suffering** for him."* – Philippians 1:29 (author's emphasis)

Many may shout out, "Ah, that kind of suffering is to do with being persecuted for our faith". I will show in the next chapter many of the ways that we can suffer in our faith, not just by means of persecution. The scriptures that I cite there will show very clearly that suffering is part of our lot when we become a follower of Christ. We should not view suffering as something that we ought to be rid of as fast as possible; as something that should not be happening to us. The deepest of faith can be brought forth in the crucible of suffering. If we personally try to avoid it or hastily want rid of it, or we have church ministers who pray over us and insist that God remove our suffering immediately, much of God's life-transforming work in us may not come to fruition. Our attitude to suffering can prevent God from fulfilling His plan in our life, and in the life of others.

"Do you Want to Get Well?"

I have had these words quoted to me on several occasions. These are words which Jesus spoke, (see John 5:6) but many use them like a weapon of condemnation against you for still not being healed after all the years they have prayed for you. This often comes from people who feel the need to say things to 'fix' the person whose healing hasn't happened, who may silently think that the sufferer doesn't really want to get well, or that they haven't searched the scriptures to find out all the ways that people in the Bible were healed.

I have longed and yearned to get well from all these conditions for all of the 27 years that I have been a Christian, and I would like to list below all the biblical actions that I personally have undertaken in faith throughout my life in Christ, in my longing and my hope for healing.

1. In faith, I went through several sessions with trained people in a local church, going through the exhausting experience of praying specific prayers to expose and cut off any generational curses and soul ties from past sins.

2. In faith, I have spent immense amounts of time confessing and repenting of all my sins; those in my pre-Christ life and all those that I have fallen into as a believer. God has forgiven me of all of these because His word says that He will, in 1 John 1:8-9.

3. In faith, I have re-enacted the actions of the woman in Mark 5:25-34, who pressed through the crowd to touch just the hem of Jesus' garment so that she could be healed.

4. In faith, I have spent many hours worshipping and praising the Lord in my weariness and suffering. I have put on the 'garment of praise for the spirit of heaviness' (see Isaiah 61:3).

5. In faith, I have anointed my body with oil from Israel, and prayed in Jesus' name to be healed.

6. In faith, I have laid my own hands on my body and prayed in Jesus' name to be healed.

7. In faith, I have prayed in Jesus' name and His authority, casting out any demons that may be affecting my body. On one occasion a demon did come out of me and it was a deeply distressing experience.

8. In the Book of Job, God restored to Job all that he had lost (which would have included his health) **when Job prayed for his friends** (see Job 40:10). So, in faith, I made a huge folder of things to pray about for all the friends I had, and I prayed for every one of them.

9. In faith, I have taken practical measures to protect our home, anointing the window frames and doorframes with oil, and then praying in each room of the house commanding any evil spirits to flee in Jesus' name.

10. In faith, I have also gone into every room of the house and removed every item, ornament, book, CD or DVD that could have a possible connection to the kingdom of darkness that I may not have been aware of, particularly souvenirs from foreign countries. I have then heaped up these things and burned them on a bonfire in the garden, reminiscent of the believers in Ephesus in Acts 19:19, who confessed their sinful practices and burned all the books that were a part of their life before they gave their lives to Christ.

There are more things that I have done in faith to help bring about my healing. Each time I have taken any steps, asking God for healing, I then leave it with God to do as He wills. He has seen me undertake these things and He has seen my faith, whether as small as a mustard seed or as large as a mountain.

Having done all that I know how to do, biblically, and still finding that my healing hasn't happened, it becomes evident to me that I must walk through this suffering for a purpose that only God knows about in full, and He may only show to me in-part in this life, but which He will reveal to me fully in glory. This side of heaven, what I **will not do** is argue with God. No matter how painful the journey of suffering is, I will walk though it with Jesus.

To those who are at odds with the reality of long-term suffering that can be a part of the life of followers of Christ, I would like to encourage you to read the following scriptures from God's word, and humbly ask if you would be able to seek the Lord so that He may reveal to you any areas that may need a change of heart towards those who suffer. Begin to put into practice any changes that He shows you, as a service to Him, and for the benefit of those in your congregations whose healings haven't happened. It will bring much joy and blessing to them as they journey in their own walk down

'Weary Lane', until that blessed day that we are all waiting for ... the Day of Redemption.

Here are some important but necessary verses from God's word:

"What sorrow awaits the leaders of my people—the shepherds of my sheep—for they have destroyed and scattered the very ones they were expected to care for," says the LORD." – Jeremiah 23:1

"You have not taken care of the weak. You have not tended the sick or bound up the injured. You have not gone looking for those who have wandered away and are lost. Instead, you have ruled them with harshness and cruelty." – Ezekiel 34:4

"I have no one else like Timothy, who genuinely cares about your welfare. **All the others care only for themselves and not for what matters to Jesus Christ.**" – Philippians 2:20-21 (author's emphasis)

"Share each other's burdens, and in this way obey the law of Christ. **If you think you are too important to help someone, you are only fooling yourself. You are not that important.**" – Galatians 6:2-3 (author's emphasis)

"And now, a word to you who are elders in the churches. I, too, am an elder and a witness to the sufferings of Christ. And I, too, will share in his glory when he is revealed to the whole world. As a fellow elder, I appeal to you: **Care for the flock that God has entrusted to you. Watch over it willingly, not grudgingly—not for what you will get out of it,** *but because you are eager to serve God.* **Don't lord it over the people assigned to your care,** *but lead them by your own good example."* – 1 Peter 5:1-3 (author's emphasis)

"If, however, you are [really] fulfilling the royal law according to the Scripture, "YOU SHALL LOVE YOUR NEIGHBOR AS YOURSELF **[that is, if you have an unselfish concern for others and do things for their benefit]**" *you are doing well.* **But if you show partiality [prejudice, favoritism], you are committing sin** *and are convicted by the Law as offenders."* – James 2:8-9 AMP (author's emphasis)

In relation to the individual members of the body of Christ, Paul says that those who are weaker are absolutely necessary in the Church, and they should be given the greater honour. I have highlighted some important parts in this passage below.

"But quite the contrary, **the parts of the body that seem to be weaker are [absolutely] necessary; and as for those parts of the body which we consider less honorable, these we treat with greater honor;** *and our less presentable parts are treated with greater modesty, while our more presentable parts do not require it.* **But God has combined the [whole] body, giving greater honor to that part which lacks it, so that there would be no division or discord in the body [that is, lack of adaptation of the parts to each other], but that the parts may have the same concern for one another. And if one member suffers, all the parts share the suffering; if one member is honored, all rejoice with it."** – 1 Corinthians 12:22-26 AMP (author's emphasis)

When we look around the Church today, there seems to be a lack of adaptation of the various parts one to another. The weaker ones seem to be overlooked in favour of the ones who seem physically stronger and more able. Emphasis seems to be placed on pushing to the forefront those who can achieve the more visible things for our churches and communities, because of their physical ability to get the jobs done on our church agenda.

But this passage says that we should have the **same** concern **one for another,** so if someone is struggling physically, all parts of the body of Christ should share in that person's suffering. We should not be doing anything that would make them feel that we have only given them the barest minimum of care that we can spare. We should be helping those who continue to suffer; helping them to use the gifts that God has put in them to fulfil His purposes in **their** lives, **in the midst** of their suffering.

Now let's look at some scriptures that will encourage us to truly love and serve those whose healings haven't happened.

"Therefore become imitators of God [copy Him and follow His example], as well-beloved children [imitate their father]; and walk continually in love [that is, value one another—practice empathy and compassion, unselfishly seeking the best for others]..." – Ephesians 5:1-2(a) AMP

"No one hates his own body but feeds and cares for it, just as Christ cares for the church. And we are members of his body." – Ephesians 5:29-30

"Be an example to all believers in what you say, in the way you live, in your love, your faith, and your purity." – 1 Timothy 4:12

"Brothers and sisters... Encourage those who are timid. Take tender care of those who are weak. Be patient with everyone." – 1 Thessalonians 5:14

"For God is not unjust. He will not forget how hard you have worked for him and how you have shown your love to him by caring for other believers, as you still do. Our great desire is that you will keep on loving others as long as life lasts..." – Hebrews 6: 10-11ᵃ

"and let us consider [thoughtfully] how we may encourage one another to love and to do good deeds..." – Hebrews 10:24 AMP

"Now you can have real love for everyone because your souls have been cleansed from selfishness and hatred when you trusted Christ to save you; so see to it that you really do love each other warmly, with all your hearts." – 1 Peter 1:22 TLB

"Finally, all of you be like-minded [united in spirit], sympathetic, brotherly, kindhearted [courteous and compassionate toward each other as members of one household], and humble in spirit;" – 1 Peter 3:8 AMP

When we put all these things together and do our best to apply them, ultimately, we are serving and honouring the Lord (see Matthew 25:36 & 40).

To close this chapter, I would like to include a couple of scripture verses that encourage us all, myself included, to pray for God's help in continuing to forgive those who hurt us with their words when our healings haven't happened. Although we can hope that people won't make hurtful comments, and even ask them to refrain from doing so, things may not change unless the Holy Spirit convicts them. Therefore, we must come before God and ask Him to help us endure their remarks; to strengthen and change us in the fiery trial of our suffering.

"Let us then approach God's throne of grace with confidence, so that we may receive mercy and find grace to help us in our time of need." – Hebrews 4:16 NIV

"We also pray that you will be strengthened with all his glorious power so you will have all the endurance and patience you need." – Colossians 1:11[a]

God is faithful, and He will keep His promise.

Chapter 5

Reasons for Suffering – What God's word says about it

Part One – Spiritual/Godly and Natural Reasons

*"For we know that all creation has been groaning as in the pains of childbirth right up to the present time. **And we believers also groan,** even though we have the Holy Spirit within us as a foretaste of future glory, for **we long for our bodies to be released from sin and suffering. We, too, wait with eager hope for the day when God will give us our full rights as his adopted children, including the new bodies he has promised us.**"*
Romans 8:22-23 (author's emphasis)

I would like to set the scene for this chapter with a quote from the eloquent, powerful preaching of J.C. Ryle, from his book, *Daily Readings from All Four Gospels: For Morning and Evening*. Ryle lived from 1816 -1900, and was the first Bishop of Liverpool from 1880 until his death in 1900. His evangelical ministry in the Anglican Church spanned fifty-eight years. His words below are deeply convicting; the sort of preaching we rarely hear from the pulpits of our churches today. Oh, for more preachers like Ryle, who would rise up in these troubling days.

Ryle says,

"Let us beware of murmuring under affliction. Every cross is meant to call us nearer to God. Bereavements have proved mercies. Losses have proved real gains. Sicknesses have led many to the great Physician of souls, sent them to the Bible, shut out the world, shown them their foolishness and taught them to pray." [1]

There **has** to be a purpose for all suffering, and Ryle's insight seems to have hit the nail on the head – to bring us to the feet of Jesus, undistracted, with open ears and hearts to hear His voice teaching us. So, with this in mind, I did a Bible search for everything I could think of to do with health, healing, sickness, affliction, suffering and pain.

Unsurprisingly, I found hundreds. The New Testament is filled with accounts of the miraculous healings that Jesus did. These are well known, cannot be disputed, and are written in Holy Scripture for all to see and believe. I believe them all! Jesus came to save us, and He healed many people of all sorts of ailments and diseases, including demonic possession. Sometimes He healed **all** the people who flocked to hear Him preach, and sometimes He healed **many** of them.

But sometimes Jesus healed only **one** person amongst the many. This has intrigued me for all the years that I have been a believer.

I have often wondered why the Church doesn't seem to discuss or teach on why Jesus only healed one person, but not the rest. I have never heard a sermon on this in all the years that I have been a Christian. It seems that church leaders may be afraid to handle this delicate issue. My silent thoughts on this have been, "What would all these unhealed people in the Bible have felt like, when the only One who could heal them has only healed one person, and has left the others in their suffering?" At a glance, it would seem a very strange, if not 'unloving' thing for Jesus to do, when He has the power and the authority to heal just by speaking it into being. This has left me puzzled by the mystery all these years.

But it is a biblical fact that Jesus did heal only one person out of the many. In the incident of the man who was lame for 38 years, recorded in John Chapter 5:1-15, it doesn't give us any clues as to why Jesus didn't heal any of the other sick people who were around the pool of Bethesda. He just healed this one man of his very long-term suffering. It then seems that Jesus just slipped away into the crowd that was there. The fate of the rest of the sufferers is left for us to ponder.

For the past 27 years of my life, this matter has quietly occupied a corner of my mind, and I haven't known what to do with it. But something in me has now stirred it up to the surface, and so the time has come for me to trust God that what I am writing will be of Him, and not of me.

It has to be borne in mind that suffering, whether long-term or short-term, can occur for all sorts of reasons. But it has been my experience that, by and large, the general approach of many in the Church is that the person who is suffering has either a lack of faith or unbelief in their life, or some unrepentant sin as being the cause of them not getting healed.

However, this seems to be a narrow-minded view to have. Whilst these are valid reasons, they are not the only ones. The scriptures mention several other reasons for why suffering and affliction are part of our life in Christ; many of these being for spiritual, godly and natural reasons.

Some of these reasons I illustrate below, although the list is not exhaustive. I am sure we could find plenty of other reasons for suffering if we did an extended study of the Bible on this subject, but I just wanted to highlight a handful to show that suffering is not just the result of lack of faith, unbelief or unrepentant sin in a person's life.

Persecution

Suffering will come as a result of any persecution that we are enduring for our faith. This can be from real, physical attacks, which is prevalent in many countries, and has been escalating in recent years. We can also feel deep, internal suffering in our spirit, which can sometimes manifest as physical pain, from the persecution that comes when people reject the truth of God's word and the message of salvation through faith in Jesus Christ. The heaviest weariness and suffering we may experience can come from the rejection, retaliation or the silent indifference from those closest to us. They say they 'know God' and believe in Him and His Son Jesus Christ, but state that God's word is not the only authority on salvation and eternal life. By making such a statement, they are rejecting the only path laid down in Holy Scripture by our Lord and Saviour Himself. Instead they may insist that it is their 'right' to follow any 'spiritual' path that they want, and to have the 'freedom' to create their own 'spiritual journey' when it comes to how to live their life and find their own path to heaven.

I have found it much easier to endure the suffering of persecution from people who have never professed to have **any** belief in God, than it is to endure the suffering from the resistance of those who **do** profess to believe in God but quite forcefully reject what His word says concerning what it means to be a follower of Christ. My heart has felt much pain in these situations, and my eyes have shed rivers of tears over the extent to which people will rebel against God's word, particularly when it comes to their view on how to receive salvation and eternal life in the kingdom of heaven.

This whole issue keeps me in prayer, often feeling much suffering and weakness in my body, feebly whispering a few words to God to do something supernatural in their lives that will shake them up and give them a 'Road to Damascus' experience (see Acts Chapter 9), turning them around from their self-made spiritual path that will not lead them to heaven. I plead with God to break through into their stubborn hearts; hearts that are like Adam and Eve, who listened to lies from Satan, causing them to believe that obeying God's word was somehow 'restrictive to their freedom', and that it would be more 'enlightening' for them if they followed Satan's version of God's word instead. I share something further on this at the back of the book, as it's an important topic that God has placed on my heart. You can find it as an Addendum, titled 'Salvation and Eternal Life'.

The way we feel when we suffer from persecution seems akin to how Paul felt in the two scriptures below. I realise that Paul is talking to faithful believers in these verses, but I do feel that the suffering he mentions will be something we will experience when we attempt to share the Gospel with those who respond with rejection or even hostility to the message that we preach.

"So I am willing to endure anything if it will bring salvation and eternal glory in Christ Jesus to those God has chosen." – 2 Timothy 2:10

"I am glad when I suffer for you in my body, for I am participating in the sufferings of Christ that continue for his body, the church. God has given me the responsibility of serving his church by proclaiming his entire message to you." – Colossians 1:24

Those verses remind us that suffering for endeavouring to preach the Gospel message of salvation through faith in Jesus Christ, which will save people from hell, is something that we must expect. Jesus suffered the ultimate persecution for preaching that all humanity needs to repent of sin and be saved in order to inherit eternal life in the kingdom of God. Jesus was mocked, whipped, spat at, and then crucified on the cross, yet He endured it knowing that it was His Father's will to go through this 'cup of suffering' in order to complete His work of salvation for all who would believe (see Matthew 26:39). So, we cannot escape the suffering that comes from being persecuted for our faith, and for our attempts at sharing the Gospel. We may not like it, but it is part of the 'job description'.

Ryle wrote a reflection upon the nature of the unconverted human heart towards believers. Here, he expresses perfectly the suffering we will also experience in the face of persecution, and the reason why:

"This is human nature appearing in its true colours. The unconverted heart hates God and will show its hatred whenever it dares and has a favourable opportunity. It will persecute God's witnesses. It will dislike all who have anything of God's mind and are renewed after his image. Why were so many of the prophets killed? Why were the names of the apostles cast out as evil by the Jews? Why were the martyrs slain? Why were so many Reformers burned? Not for any sins they had committed. They all suffered because they were godly men. And human nature, unconverted, hates godly men because it hates God…It is not the sins of the believer that the world dislikes but his goodness. It is not the remains of the old nature that call forth the world's enmity, but the exhibition of the new. Let us remember these things and be patient. The world hated Christ and the world will hate Christians." [2]

Over one-hundred years has passed since Ryle wrote those words. In our present day, we are seeing a rapid escalation of hatred and hostility towards followers of Christ. So much evil is coming upon the world, and when we boldly share the light of the Gospel message of salvation with those who are in the darkness of this world, they react like cockroaches when a light is turned on – they scurry around as fast as possible to find a place of darkness to hide themselves again.

These words in the following scripture passage sum up perfectly this reaction of those who reject God's word, and persecute us:

*"Whoever believes in him is not condemned, but whoever does not believe stands condemned already because they have not believed in the name of God's one and only Son. **This is the verdict: Light has come into the world, but people loved darkness instead of light because their deeds were evil. Everyone who does evil hates the***

light, and will not come into the light for fear that their deeds will be exposed." – John 3:18-20 NIV (author's emphasis)

But, despite the persecution we face and the suffering it causes us, let us take heart and rejoice in the knowledge that, because of our faith in Jesus, all our suffering will turn to glory when we enter into His eternal kingdom.

"Blessed are you when people insult you, persecute you and falsely say all kinds of evil against you because of me. Rejoice and be glad, because great is your reward in heaven, for in the same way they persecuted the prophets who were before you." – Matthew 5:11 NIV

"For his Spirit joins with our spirit to affirm that we are God's children. And since we are his children, we are his heirs. In fact, together with Christ we are heirs of God's glory. But if we are to share his glory, **we must also share his suffering. Yet what we suffer now is nothing compared to the glory he will reveal to us later."** – Romans 8:16-18 (author's emphasis)

"And some of the wise will fall victim to persecution. In this way, they will be refined and cleansed and made pure until the time of the end, for the appointed time is still to come." – Daniel 11:35

"...God will use this persecution to show his justice and to make you worthy of his Kingdom, for which you are suffering." – 2 Thessalonians 1:5

"Endure suffering along with me, as a good soldier of Christ Jesus." – 2 Timothy 2:3

"Yes, and everyone who wants to live a godly life in Christ Jesus will suffer persecution." – 2 Timothy 3:12

As we can see, God uses the suffering that we experience from persecution to cleanse and refine us and make us fit for His kingdom, as good soldiers of Jesus Christ. When we feel the pain of this persecution, let us fix our eyes on Jesus and on the glory that awaits us in heaven. This will comfort and strengthen us, knowing that, even though it seems that all our effort is being rejected, in God's eyes it is **not** in vain. Our effort to save souls may not appear to come to fruition in those who continue to reject it, but all our effort is actually storing up for ourselves treasure in heaven, which we will receive when we enter the gates into eternal life with Jesus.

"What blessings await you when people hate you and exclude you and mock you and curse you as evil because you follow the Son of Man. When that happens, be happy! Yes, leap for joy! For a great reward awaits you in heaven. And remember, their ancestors treated the ancient prophets that same way." – Luke 6:22-24

And finally, let us remind ourselves of the persecution that Jesus endured, so that in the persecution we face for our faith in Christ, we will be able to draw strength from Him not to give up when we feel overcome with weariness.

"...[looking away from all that will distract us and] focusing our eyes on Jesus, who is the Author and Perfecter of faith [the first incentive for our belief and the One who brings our faith to maturity], who for the joy [of accomplishing the goal] set before Him endured the cross, disregarding the shame, and sat down at the right hand of the throne of God [revealing His deity, His authority, and the completion of His work]. **Just consider and meditate on Him who endured from sinners such bitter hostility against Himself [consider it all in comparison with your trials], so that you will not grow weary and lose heart.**" - Hebrews 12:2-3 AMP (author's emphasis)

Spiritual Attack

Our suffering could be the result of spiritual attacks coming at us from the kingdom of darkness, from Satan and his demons. Whenever we undertake anything for God's kingdom, Satan is there in the background waiting to pounce on us in an effort to trip us up and make us feel defeated. Once we become a follower of Christ, we become Satan's target. Satan is not interested in bothering nonbelievers, because those who do not believe in Jesus Christ as their Lord and Saviour already belong to Satan (whether they are aware of it or not). Satan is hell-bent on attacking all who have given their lives to Christ, who, by their faith in Jesus Christ as their Lord and Saviour, have been transferred from Satan's kingdom of darkness into Jesus' kingdom of Light.

As Christians, we have to realise that Satan is out to get us, and his attacks will be relentless. Night and day, we have to be on our guard against all the wiles of the wicked one. We must be ready with our spiritual armour on, at all times, ever watchful for the sudden pounce of the roaring lion who is looking for someone to devour (see 1 Peter 5:8).

The very thought of this relentless battle is enough to make us feel weary and exhausted! We are soldiers of Christ, having to wear our armour 24 hours a day, 7 days a week, 365 days a year… until He returns. Imagine an army soldier having to wear his heavy protective armour day and night for a whole year, and for his own safety never being able to take it off! Now imagine that whole year being for the rest of the soldier's life. Imagine how physically exhausted he would feel having to wear his armour until he dies, simply to protect himself from his earthly enemy.

Now put this into perspective in our spiritual war against Satan and his demons. They are not a figment of our imagination! God's word tells us plainly that they are **very** real, and that we **must** be on guard at all times for their next onslaught. Constantly being ready for something that may happen places the body in a state of permanent 'semi-alert'. In normal everyday life, when we are faced with something that is stressful or threatening, this causes adrenaline to pump through our bodies, in order for us to be able to react to the situation in a fight or flight mode. After the incident has subsided, our adrenaline then drops down to a normal, safe level.

But in our Christian life, we are required to live our lives in a ready, on-guard, semi-alert state at **all times** against our adversary. This means that, subconsciously, our adrenaline is permanently raised so that we are ready to do battle with the kingdom of darkness when it hurls itself at us. Anyone in the medical profession will tell you that being in a situation where your adrenaline is permanently raised will produce exhaustion. So, as followers of Christ, having to wear our spiritual armour all the time and be on guard against the onslaughts of the kingdom of darkness 24/7/365, is it any wonder that so many followers of Christ are suffering long-term weariness, exhaustion and physical pain?

"For we are not fighting against flesh-and-blood enemies, but against evil rulers and authorities of the unseen world, against mighty powers in this dark world, and against evil spirits in the heavenly places. Therefore, put on every piece of God's armor so you will be able to resist the enemy in the time of evil. Then after the battle you will still be standing firm." – Ephesians 6:12-13

"For every child of God defeats this evil world, and we achieve this victory through our faith. And who can win this battle against the world? Only those who believe that Jesus is the Son of God." – 1 John 5:4-5

"For though we walk in the flesh [as mortal men], we are not carrying on our [spiritual] warfare according to the flesh and using the weapons of man. The weapons of our warfare are not physical [weapons of flesh and blood]. Our weapons are divinely powerful for the destruction of fortresses. We are destroying sophisticated arguments and every exalted and proud thing that sets itself up against the [true] knowledge of God..." – 2 Corinthians 10:4-5a AMP

"Dear friends, don't be surprised at the fiery trials you are going through, as if something strange were happening to you. Instead, be very glad—for these trials make you partners with Christ in his suffering, so that you will have the wonderful joy of seeing his glory when it is revealed to all the world." – 1 Peter 4:12-13

Therefore, let us be ever mindful that the heaviness we feel is akin to what Jesus endured when He was led by the Holy Spirit into the wilderness to be tested by Satan, who used and twisted the word of God itself as a means to spiritually attack Jesus. This is an example of suffering by God's permitted will (which we will look at in the next section) which even Jesus, the Son of God, had to accept and endure in order to be able to undertake and fulfil His ministry of salvation, after He had come out of the wilderness (see Matthew 4:1-17).

Whilst the spiritual attacks that come against us are not on the scale of what Jesus endured, they are still painful to us. We can take comfort in the knowledge that He went through intense suffering for God's purposes, and because of this He is able to help us and strengthen us in our own times of weariness from spiritual attacks.

For an excellent explanation of the real battle that Christians face from Satan and his demons on a daily basis, I would like to encourage you to read my husband's book, *The Christian Book for Men – Biblical Solutions to the Battles Facing Men,* (in particular, Volume One, Chapter 3). I have listed it in the Recommended Reading section, and details about it can be viewed on his website www.thechristianbookformen.com. Whilst his book is primarily addressed to Christian men, I am sure it will help women as well to fully understand the beings in the spiritual realm that rage against all who are faithful followers of Christ.

God's Permitted Suffering

There is a suffering that we can experience which is by God's permitted will, and it is always for His purposes.

Many in the Church struggle with the biblical truth that God can permit suffering to come into the lives of those who believe in Him. Yet I would like to point to two separate stories in the Bible where God permitted suffering, both for a purpose.

The first account is in John Chapter 9, where Jesus saw a man who was blind from birth, and His disciples asked Him a question that was so direct, it is the sort of thing many sufferers hear today when they struggle with long-term health conditions. Here is the passage, with the disciples' assumptive, indirect accusation highlighted:

"Now as Jesus passed by, He saw a man who was blind from birth. **And His disciples asked Him, saying, "Rabbi, who sinned, this man or his parents, that he was born blind?"** *Jesus answered, "Neither this man nor his parents sinned, but that the works of God should be revealed in him..."* – John 9:1-3 (author's emphasis)

The **believers** who were walking with Jesus **automatically assumed** that sin was the cause of this man's blindness. Jesus quickly corrected their wrong thinking by stating that the man had been born blind in order that God's mighty power would be revealed at that moment. Jesus then healed the man of his blindness. Although the story doesn't tell us how old the blind man was, what we take away from it is an understanding that God allowed this man to suffer and wait many years for his healing. People in the Church today tend to focus on the miraculous healing in this account, but seem to avoid the fact that **God permitted him to suffer** blindness for such a long time before healing him.

The second story is a much-used favourite from the Old Testament. It is the story of Job. Whenever I have heard sermons on this, again the main focus is on how amazing God is to have restored to Job much more than he lost in his time of suffering. But I cannot recall hearing any sermons that address the fact that it was God (yes, God!) who permitted Satan to come against Job and wreak havoc in his life. Job was a righteous man with whom God was pleased; his suffering was not due to any sin. Yet **God gave Satan permission** to afflict Job with immense suffering and loss, in order to prove to Satan that Job would not lose faith in God, nor curse God, even though he had lost everything except his own life.

The full story of what God permitted Job to suffer is written in the Book of Job Chapters 1 & 2. But below, I want to highlight the passage where Satan attacked Job's health.

"Then the LORD asked Satan, "Have you noticed my servant Job? He is the finest man in all the earth. He is blameless—a man of complete integrity. He fears God and stays away from evil. And he has maintained his integrity, even though you urged me to harm him without cause." Satan replied to the LORD, "Skin for skin! A man will give up everything he has to save his life. But reach out and take away his health, and he will surely curse you to your face!" **"All right, do with him as you please," the LORD said to Satan.** *"But spare his life." So Satan left the LORD's presence, and he struck Job with terrible boils from head to foot."* – Job 2:3-7 (author's emphasis)

Here is Job's response to his suffering:

"At least I can take comfort in this: **Despite the pain, I have not denied the words of the Holy One.***"* – Job 6:10 (author's emphasis)

His friends also told him that his catastrophic losses and suffering were the result of some sin that he must have committed, and that his health would return once he repented.

Here is one of the passages:

"If only you would prepare your heart and lift up your hands to him in prayer! Get rid of your sins, and leave all iniquity behind you. Then your face will brighten with innocence. You will be strong and free of fear. You will forget your misery; it will be like water flowing away. Your life will be brighter than the noonday." – Job 11:13-17[a]

In relation to their accusations, Job cries out:

"I am innocent, but they call me a liar. My suffering is incurable, though I have not sinned." – Job 34:6 (author's emphasis)

Even though they accused Job of sinning, his friend Elihu gave a valid reason for God permitting suffering:

"But **by means of their suffering**, *he rescues those who suffer.*

*For **he gets their attention through adversity**."* – Job 36:15 (author's emphasis)

The apostle James also points us to Job, and the honour that is to be given to those who endure under the hand of God's permitted suffering:

*"For examples of patience in suffering, dear brothers and sisters, look at the prophets who spoke in the name of the Lord. **We give great honor to those who endure under suffering.** For instance, you know about Job, a man of great endurance. You can see how the Lord was kind to him at the end, for the Lord is full of tenderness and mercy."* – James 5:10-11 (author's emphasis)

In both of the stories above, neither the man born blind nor Job had sinned, yet they were both greatly afflicted for God's purposes **by the permitted will of God Himself**. How many of us can truly say that we consider other people's suffering as something that God has permitted into their lives? Rather, how many of us may treat those who suffer in the same manner that the disciples did regarding the blind man, as if his blindness was due to sin?

Today, I wonder how many thousands of Christ-followers are enduring long-term suffering, not because of sin but because God is allowing it to test their faith? Of this number, I also wonder how many of their Christian friends say something similar to these words of Job's friends? Brothers and sisters, let's not automatically jump to conclusions like Job's friends did. It won't be helpful for the person who's suffering.

The Prophet Isaiah also endured sickness, which God permitted into his life:

*"My eyes grew tired of looking to heaven for help. I am in trouble, Lord. Help me!" But what could I say? **For he himself sent this sickness. Now I will walk humbly throughout my years because of this anguish I have felt.**"* – Isaiah 38:14[b] – 15 (author's emphasis)

The Psalmist wrote:

"I know, O LORD, that Your judgments are right,
And that in faithfulness You have afflicted me.
Let, I pray, Your merciful kindness be for my comfort,
According to Your word to Your servant." – Psalm 119:74-76 NKJV
(author's emphasis)

Let's look at the example of Jesus in the garden of Gethsemane: it was God's permitted will that Jesus should suffer and die for the salvation of mankind, but in desperation He cried out to God for another way out of the suffering, showing His human nature. (Jesus understands how we feel!) If God permitted suffering in the life of His only Son, then surely it follows that it can be God's will for our life too? Let us learn from Jesus' response, though:

"He went a little farther and fell on His face, and prayed, saying,
*"O My Father, if it is possible, let this cup pass from Me; **nevertheless,***
not as I will, but as You will." – Matthew 26:39

In fact, the following scripture confirms that we likewise will endure the same, and that Jesus is able to help us in these situations:

"Since he himself has gone through suffering and testing, he is able
to help us when we are being tested." – Hebrews 2:18

God's permitted suffering puts us in a place where He is able to do His much-needed work in us, to transform us into the likeness of Christ. Seeing as we are but flesh, such a work in us is not going to be a quick, painless job! Our spirit is willing to be like Christ, but our flesh is weak (Matthew 26:4ᵇ), and the struggle we go through, between wanting to obey God's word and wanting to remain as we are in our natural flesh, can be enormous.

"And not only this, but [with joy] let us exult in our sufferings
and rejoice in our hardships, knowing that hardship (distress,
pressure, trouble) produces patient endurance; and endurance,
proven character (spiritual maturity); and proven character, hope
and confident assurance [of eternal salvation]. Such hope [in God's
promises] never disappoints us,..." – Romans 5:3-5ᵃ AMP

Let us conclude then, that when God permits suffering to come into our lives, whether that be short-term or long-term, He is bringing it to us for a purpose. If it is because of sin, then it may be to teach us something that He has tried to gently convict us about several times before, which we have ignored, but now He is having to take us into adversity and suffering so that, at last, we will listen to Him and obey Him.

"Though the Lord gave you adversity for food and suffering for drink, he will still be with you to teach you. You will see your teacher with your own eyes. Your own ears will hear him. Right behind you a voice will say, "This is the way you should go," – Isaiah 30:20-21

If we have not sinned, but He has permitted suffering to come into our lives, then let us do as Job did, and remain faithful to God in the midst of our suffering, and not curse Him.

The Refiner's Fire

Our suffering could be the result of God taking us through a period in the 'Refiner's Fire', to purge out the sinful flesh in us and change us into the image of Christ, so that we begin to think, speak and act according to God's word in all situations, rather than from our knee-jerk reactions that come from our old pre-Christ habits.

In God's refining fire of suffering, He will reveal to us all that is in us that is not pleasing in His sight. He will search and test our hearts, unearthing the real motives that are behind our inward thoughts and our outward actions. Nothing is hidden from the eyes of the Lord, and He will not let us escape His refining process. The purpose of this is ultimately for our good, although the process itself will most likely be very excruciating. God's refining process is to test us so that our faith is purified and is shown to be genuine.

"My suffering was good for me, for it taught me to pay attention to your decrees. Your instructions are more valuable to me than millions in gold and silver." – Psalm 119:71-72

"I have refined you, but not as silver is refined. Rather, I have refined you in the furnace of suffering." – Isaiah 48:10

"He knows about everyone, everywhere. Everything about us is bare and wide open to the all-seeing eyes of our living God; nothing can be hidden from him to whom we must explain all that we have done." – Hebrews 4:13 TLB

The Passion Translation puts the above verse as follows:

"There is not one person who can hide their thoughts from God, for nothing that we do remains a secret, and nothing created is concealed, but everything is exposed and defenseless before his eyes, to whom we must render an account." – Hebrews 4:13 TPT

The writer to the Hebrews has this to say about the importance of godly correction:

"And have you forgotten the encouraging words God spoke to you as his children? He said, "My child, don't make light of the LORD's discipline, and don't give up when he corrects you. For the LORD disciplines those he loves, and he punishes each one he accepts as his child." As you endure this divine discipline, remember that God is treating you as his own children." – Hebrews 12:4-7[a]

As nothing evil, wicked, sinful and unholy will be allowed to enter into God's kingdom, God's ultimate purpose for His children enduring the suffering of His refining fire is because of the wonderful joy that awaits us in His kingdom. In order for us to be counted worthy of entering in, everything that is in our life that would prevent our being received into His kingdom **must** be purged out of us. The burning up of all the ways of the flesh that we cling to, which is not pleasing in God's sight, will increase more and more, especially if we are resisting His refining process. He **will** refine us, whether we like it or not, and this will intensify as we hasten ever nearer to the Day of Christ's return.

"There is wonderful joy ahead, even though you must endure many trials for a little while. These trials will show that your faith

is genuine. It is being tested as fire tests and purifies gold—though your faith is far more precious than mere gold. So when your faith remains strong through many trials, it will bring you much praise and glory and honor on the day when Jesus Christ is revealed to the whole world." – 1 Peter 1:6-7

And in relation to the Day of His return, Jesus exhorts us to be watchful of the signs of the End Times, and to live our lives making ourselves ready to be taken up in glory with Him (see Matthew Chapter 24). So, let us not be rebellious children when He is purifying us. Let us humbly submit to His correction, knowing that the time is now urgent, and that Day which we so long for is getting closer with each passing second.

"This is all the more urgent, for you know how late it is; time is running out. Wake up, for our salvation is nearer now than when we first believed. The night is almost gone; the day of salvation will soon be here. So remove your dark deeds like dirty clothes, and put on the shining armor of right living." – Romans 13:11-12

Prayer and Intercession

When we are in times of prayer and intercession, as the Lord places in our hearts a deep burden for the things that He wants us to pray for, we can experience physical pain in our bodies. I have had this happen to me many times. I may be quietly resting on my bed, worshipping the Lord and asking Him to reveal to me what is on His heart, when, all of a sudden, I will be overwhelmed with weeping for something that I know nothing about. I will cry out to God to show me what my tears are about, and gradually I will start praying for something that was never in my thoughts at all. Often my tears have felt like the Lord is allowing me to experience His own weeping for the lost. I have felt a fear of great foreboding, accompanied by a kind of panic and deep grief for people in the world who would rather remain in the darkness of this world than repent and come into the kingdom of Light and be saved. At times, the burdens that the Lord places in my heart are so intense that all I am able to do is offer up a prayer of deep groaning, because any actual words of prayer seem to be totally inadequate. Paul sums this up well in the following verses:

"In the same way the Spirit [comes to us and] helps us in our weakness. We do not know what prayer to offer or how to offer it as we should, but the Spirit Himself [knows our need and at the right time] intercedes on our behalf with sighs and groanings too deep for words. And He who searches the hearts knows what the mind of the Spirit is, because the Spirit intercedes [before God] on behalf of God's people in accordance with God's will." – Romans 8:26-27 AMP

None of us will have experienced the immense physical agony that Jesus endured in the Garden of Gethsemane, prior to His crucifixion, but the following scripture gives us an example of the extent to which the human body can display symptoms of suffering whilst in intense prayer and intercession.

"He prayed more fervently, and he was in such agony of spirit that his sweat fell to the ground like great drops of blood." – Luke 22:44

When God took me through an intense time of physical suffering in 2011 where all I could do was pray like never-before, it felt like a raging fire was burning inside me for two weeks, causing sweat to pour out of me night and day. It did not subside until God's work was complete. The story of this is in Chapter 6.

Living in this Fallen World

There are two main areas that I would like to mention under this section; the first of these being:

a) Sickness

Concerning suffering, it seems to be an overlooked fact that it can occur simply because we now live in a 'fallen world' following Adam and Eve's rebellion against God in the Garden of Eden. The result of their sin of disobedience against God's word means that sickness and suffering entered into the world and have become part of life for all humanity. Followers of Christ are not exempt from it! We cannot avoid it, and we will occasionally get sick and suffer from natural earthly causes now and again.

As I have mentioned before, over the years, I have heard many Christians say things like, "It is not God's will for you to be unwell or to suffer". Having scoured the scriptures on the subject of suffering and pain, of whatever kind it may be, I have found a very different view on this throughout the Bible.

A scan through the Old Testament will show the reality that many of the children of Israel, who were God's people, got sick during their life on this earth, so why would we make such claims that it is not God's will for us to be sick or to suffer? I am sure God doesn't want us to end up being ill, but that is a very different thing to claiming that it is not His will for us to be ill. I believe that such claims are very shaky ground to stand on, in light of the scripture below. These words are spoken by Jesus Himself directly to His followers:

*"In the world you have tribulation and **distress and suffering**, but be courageous [be confident, be undaunted, be filled with joy]; I have overcome the world." [My conquest is accomplished, My victory abiding.]"* – John 16:33ᵇ AMP (author's emphasis)

This is the exact opposite of the modern church's teaching that 'it's not God's will for you to suffer'. We would do well to pay attention to what He says, and not believe, speak or teach 'spiritually-sounding' words that are contrary to His word.

Let's look at some more scriptures.

When Paul first visited the believers at Galatia, **he was sick**. There is no mention, in the passage below, of them praying for him, although we could probably assume that they would have done this. But the overriding emphasis is that they cared for him **in his**

sickness, and **did not despise him or turn him away.**

"Surely you remember that I was sick when I first brought you the Good News. But even though my condition tempted you to reject me, ***you did not despise me or turn me away.*** *No, you took me in and* ***cared for me as though I were an angel from God or even Christ Jesus himself."*** – Galatians 4 :13-14 (author's emphasis)

This same passage in the New International Version uses different words to describe how he was treated by his fellow believers. These words, which I have highlighted, emphasise well the issue that I raised in the previous chapter; that those who are sick or in suffering can be scorned by those who are well:

"As you know, it was because of an illness that I first preached the gospel to you, and even though my illness was a trial to you, ***you did not treat me with contempt or scorn.*** *Instead, you welcomed me as if I were an angel of God, as if I were Christ Jesus himself."*

Do we treat our fellow believers who are sick and suffering as if they were Christ Himself?

Timothy was frequently unwell, but in the verse below, Paul doesn't even mention prayer. He just gave Timothy a very simple instruction!

"Don't drink only water. You ought to drink a little wine for the sake of your stomach because you are sick so often." – 1 Timothy 5:23

Whilst on his travels, Paul said that he left another believer behind because he was ill. The context in the Bible doesn't mention any care for this man, but we should assume that he was taken care of by others whilst Paul was on his trip preaching the Gospel.

"Erastus stayed at Corinth, and I left Trophimus sick at Miletus." – 2 Timothy 4:20

And whilst in prison, Paul wrote the following about Epaphroditus:

"Meanwhile, I thought I should send Epaphroditus back to you.

*He is a true brother, co-worker, and fellow soldier. And he was your messenger to help me in my need. I am sending him because he has been longing to see you, and he was very distressed that **you heard he was ill. And he certainly was ill; in fact, he almost died.**"* – Philippians 2:25-27ᵃ (author's emphasis)

Many of the Psalms have much to say about sickness, too, and can be a source of comfort to us in our ill health:

*"The LORD sustains them **on their sickbed** and restores them from their bed of illness."* – Psalm 41:3 NIV (author's emphasis)

*"Whom have I in heaven but you? I desire you more than anything on earth. **My health may fail, and my spirit may grow weak,** but God remains the strength of my heart; he is mine forever."* – Psalm 73:25-26 (author's emphasis)

*"Seventy years are given to us! Some even live to eighty. **But even the best years are filled with pain and trouble...**"* – Psalm 90:10 (author's emphasis)

The following is an amazing passage describing the suffering of our earthly bodies whilst we yearn for our new glorified bodies:

"Though our bodies are dying, our spirits are being renewed every day. For our present troubles are small and won't last very long. Yet they produce for us a glory that vastly outweighs them and will last forever! So we don't look at the troubles we can see now; rather, we fix our gaze on things that cannot be seen. For the things we see now will soon be gone, but the things we cannot see will last forever. For we know that when this earthly tent we live in is taken down (that is, when we die and leave this earthly body), we will have a house in heaven, an eternal body made for us by God himself and not by human hands. We grow weary in our present bodies, and we long to put on our heavenly bodies like new clothing. For we will put on heavenly bodies; we will not be spirits without bodies. While we live in these earthly bodies, we groan and sigh, but it's not that we want to

die and get rid of these bodies that clothe us. Rather, we want to put on our new bodies so that these dying bodies will be swallowed up by life. God himself has prepared us for this, and as a guarantee he has given us his Holy Spirit." – 2 Corinthians 4:16-18, 5:1-5

Paul also writes,

*"And we believers also groan, even though we have the Holy Spirit within us as a foretaste of future glory, **for we long for our bodies to be released from sin and suffering.** We, too, wait with eager hope for the day when God will give us our full rights as his adopted children, including the new bodies he has promised us."* – Romans 8:23 (author's emphasis)

So, let's accept that God's word is quite clear that we may get sick from time to time in our earthly bodies, and that our flesh will grow old and weary as we draw closer to our death.

God has created our bodies in such intricate detail that many ailments will simply heal naturally. As Christians, we ought to see that this is actually God working an **incredible** miracle in us.

Every healing is a miracle… not just the ones that are instant.

b) Neglect and Abuse

Another area of suffering due to living in this fallen world is that, as imperfect people, we may find ourselves in family relationships that are difficult, fractured and broken, sometimes beyond repair, despite all our biblical efforts to bring about a resolution and restoration.

We may have experienced the effects of other people sinning against us in the form of neglect or abuse, verbally, emotionally or physically and/or mentally usually from people we know who are close to us; relatives, friends, neighbours, school teachers, colleagues and employers. We may have been powerless to do anything about these situations.

This is a vast subject, and not being a trained counsellor, it is not something that I am qualified to give any advice on, other than to share my own experience of being on the receiving end of physical and emotional abuse.

As a child, I received unwanted physical attention from two people, which made me feel uncomfortable, anxious and frightened, and I didn't know what to do about it.

When I was a teenager, I was verbally attacked and physically threatened by a gang of youths whilst I was making a call from a phone-box on the street.

When I started work, I was a target of unwanted sexual harassment, which got ignored by my employer. At another place of work, I was the subject of intimidation by a colleague whilst I was pregnant. I was frightened to go to work each day, and the intimidation caused me so much distress that my doctor signed me off work for the remainder of my pregnancy, to protect my health and the life of my unborn baby.

I have been in situations where I have been physically grabbed and almost pushed down the stairs, and one time a person had their hands around my throat, and I had to kick them hard to get them off me.

My heart goes out to every person who is reading this book, who has experienced any kind of neglect or abuse at any time in their life.

Many people in the Church may be suffering physical, mental and emotional pain from neglect and abuse, from the past or even ongoing situations. Many are afraid to speak about their trauma, and as such, the circumstances are internalised, resulting in suffering.

Whenever we are in the presence of anyone who suffers from long-term conditions, let us always be mindful that unspeakable abuse may have been, or may still be a part of their life, which they may never be able to verbalise. Let us love them with acts of kindness, which can bring a measure of support, comfort and emotional healing to them, even though their physical and mental sufferings may remain.

The End Times – Satan 'Wearing out the Saints'

The subject of the heading of this section is one spiritual reason why many in the Church could be suffering from chronic exhaustion when all medical tests have drawn a blank. Over the past few years, many Christians have said to me that, all of a sudden, a great weariness and exhaustion has come upon them, the likes of which they have never experienced before. After having made healthy changes to their lives to reflect a better work/life balance, a good diet and more exercise, still this weariness doesn't seem to lift and is all-consuming. Somehow, they are managing to pull themselves through each day, but they just cannot seem to overcome this exhaustion.

This term, 'wearing out the saints' is taken from Daniel 7:25. Many may have read this verse but not fully understood the physical implications of it. In that verse (see below) Daniel was given a dramatic vision of the End Times, which included 'wearing out' the saints; the faithful followers of Jesus. Those saints who are alive at the time that this vision is fulfilled will experience this great 'wearing out', caused by the spirit of the antichrist working through organisations, institutions and earthly bodies that have rejected God. Anyone who has rejected God becomes the devil's 'playground', and slowly but surely Satan will twist all that God has created, and with great guile he will persuade the world that it is time for a 'change'.

"And he shall speak words against the Most High [God] **and shall wear out the saints** *of the Most High and think to* **change** *the time [of sacred feasts and holy days] and the law;"* – Daniel 7:25 AMPCE (author's emphasis)

The Living Bible renders this verse as follows:

"He will defy the Most High God and wear down the saints with persecution, and he will try to change all laws, morals, and customs."

When we read these two translations together, it would seem that we could well be in this period right now, or at least in the beginnings of it: secular authorities are trying to change or do away with the laws, morals, customs and sacred feasts that have stood in society for millennia. I would say that the laws, morals and customs are the Christian beliefs and values upon which many nations have been founded, and shockingly the secular authorities are now putting pressure upon the Church to change. This results in the Church bringing in deceptive teaching to please society. All of this is happening on an almost global scale. Interestingly, I have noticed that this increase in weariness which has come upon followers of Christ seems to have coincided with the increase in the attempts by those in positions of national authority to assert godless agendas into every area of society.

If we are true believers, obeying God's word and doing all that we can to live a life that is worthy of God's calling, we will most definitely feel the immense burden of this rapid decline. The enormity of it can make us feel powerless to do anything about it. It will feel as though our spirits are being crushed under the weight of the world's ungodliness and increasing lawlessness, and the Church's apostasy, rebellion and unrepentant sin.

During these troubling times, we must continue to hope and trust in the Lord, knowing that He has got it all in hand, and our 'time of departure' from this earth is drawing ever nearer. If we are faithful, obedient followers of Christ, He will not forsake us and leave us here on earth to experience His wrath (see Luke 21:34-36 on this, which I have listed a few paragraphs ahead).

On this subject, I would like to shed some light on this, particularly in view of the increasing rejection of God's word and His holy laws which is happening within the Church in our times. The following scriptures give a serious warning to us, which ought to bring conviction, confession and repentance, with the purpose of getting right with God.

"Let no one deceive you with empty arguments [that encourage you to sin], for because of these things the wrath of God comes upon the sons of disobedience [those who habitually sin]." – Ephesians 5:6 AMP

"Be careful that you do not refuse to listen to the One who is speaking. For if the people of Israel did not escape when they refused to listen to Moses, the earthly messenger, we will certainly not escape if we reject the One who speaks to us from heaven!" – Hebrews 12:25

Talking to His followers, Jesus gave them a solemn warning about how to live whilst the 'birth pains' of the beginnings of the End Times escalate upon the earth:

"But take heed to yourselves, lest your hearts be weighed down with carousing, drunkenness, and cares of this life, and that Day come on you unexpectedly. For it will come as a snare on all those who dwell on the face of the whole earth. **Watch therefore, and pray always that you may be counted worthy to escape all these things that will come to pass, and to stand before the Son of Man."** – Luke 21:34-36 NKJV (author's emphasis)

The Living Bible translation shows Jesus expressing this passage in a more personal, direct way, giving us a clear understanding:

"Watch out! Don't let my sudden coming catch you unawares; don't let me find you living in careless ease, carousing and drinking, and occupied with the problems of this life, like all the rest of the world. Keep a constant watch. And pray that if possible you may **arrive in my presence without having to experience these horrors."** – Luke 21:34-36 TLB (author's emphasis)

To *'escape all these things that will come to pass'* means that we will be delivered from it; we will be removed from experiencing it. The second part of that verse says, *"and stand before the Son of Man."* There are two events mentioned in that sentence which are joined together by the word 'and'. It is clear to me that both events will happen simultaneously. Without a shadow of doubt in my mind, we will escape the horrors to come **and** then at the same moment be standing before Jesus. This is the clearest indication to me of the Rapture of the **faithful believers** being removed from the earth just moments before the wrath of God is poured out, **and** as soon as we are removed, we will stand before Jesus.

Paul also confirms that Jesus will rescue us from the coming wrath:

*"[look forward and confidently] wait for [the coming of] His Son from heaven, whom He raised from the dead—**Jesus, who [personally] rescues us from the coming wrath [and draws us to Himself**, granting us all the privileges and rewards of a new life with Him]."* – 1 Thessalonians 1:10 AMP (author's emphasis)

If Jesus **said it,** and Paul **confirmed it,** then I am going to **believe it!** Are you?

So, in this period of time, where we are suffering the 'wearing out of the saints', let us examine our lives and put right anything that is not in keeping with God's holy word. The time has now passed for us to still be carrying on in complacency, half-heartedness, and any sinful behaviour.

Jesus is coming back, and we do not want to be found in such a state that He considers us **unworthy** to escape the wrath that **is** to come.

To conclude this section, let us take comfort in the following passage, and in the truth that this reveals:

"We tell you this directly from the Lord: We who are still living when the Lord returns will not meet him ahead of those who have died. For the Lord himself will come down from heaven with a commanding shout, with the voice of the archangel, and with the trumpet call of God. First, the believers who have died will rise from their graves. Then, together with them, we who are still alive and

remain on the earth will be caught up in the clouds to meet the Lord in the air. Then we will be with the Lord forever. So encourage each other with these words." – 1 Thessalonians 4:15-18

Overwork and Burnout

After finishing His work of creation, **God rested** from His work (see Genesis 2:2). We know that after the fall of Adam and Eve, God cursed the ground, and it was hard work for them just to grow food so that they could eat (see Genesis 3:17).

The psalmist says that in vain we rise up early and stay up late toiling for food to eat (see Psalm 127:2).

In Ecclesiastes, Solomon says,

"In my search for wisdom and in my observation of people's burdens here on earth, I discovered that there is ceaseless activity, day and night." – Ecclesiastes 8:16

Paul says that, in relation to his work for God's kingdom,

"I have labored and toiled and have often gone without sleep." – 2 Corinthians 11:27[a] NIV

Also,

"Surely you remember, brothers and sisters, our toil and hardship; we worked night and day in order not to be a burden to anyone while we preached the gospel of God to you." – 1 Thessalonians 2:9 NIV

In the Church today, the culture seems to be that we must be constantly buzzing with 'Christian' activity, morning, noon and night, in order to appear 'successful'. This is a recipe for disaster. Working far too many hours and running ourselves ragged in order to please people and be accessible to our communities may look good, but in the long run it is not healthy. Not taking time out to restore our own bodies will cause burn-out and fatigue, which is not easily fixed with just an occasional weekend off now and again. In fact, if we have suffered any kind of emotional or physical breakdown, it can leave our immune systems very weakened, and just when we think we have rested enough and feel that we have more-or-less recovered, along comes another life event that tips us right back to where we started.

In the following scripture, we might take note that Jesus became tired and weary after walking for a long time, and He needed to sit down and rest.

*"Jacob's well was there; and **Jesus, tired** from the long walk, sat **wearily** beside the well about noontime."* – John 4:6 (author's emphasis)

If Jesus needed to rest, and we are called to follow Him, then that means doing as Jesus did – including taking time out to rest. If we don't, do we realise that we are therefore going against God's word?

We also know that Jesus often retreated into the wilderness to pray. This would be a time in His Father's presence, which would undoubtedly bring a sense of rest and restoration of energy to enable Him to come back from the wilderness to continue His ministry.

"But Jesus often withdrew to the wilderness for prayer." – Luke 5:16

I know from my own experience that, no matter how intense my times of prayer may be, I come away feeling a spiritual rest inside me.

When we have overworked our bodies, and taken hardly any time to adequately rest and restore ourselves, and have ended up with 'burnout', yes God could miraculously heal and restore our health and strength, but it is unlikely that we would learn the wisdom of how to look after our bodies properly. If God did do a miracle like this, we would probably throw ourselves right back into the frantic activity that we were doing before we crashed in a heap. Sometimes God **leaves** us in our wrecked state to discipline us, and to help us learn better ways of living; ways that are kinder to our bodies, that enable us to set healthy boundaries, and give us the courage to say "No" to the demands of others.

As Christians, we have this deep urge to want to please everybody and not let them down, even when our own bodies are screaming at us to stop! I know this from personal experience, because I have spent much of my life jumping in to help all and sundry the very moment that I see a need. I do the job, but with each effort, I am finding that my body takes much longer to recover from the exertion. It has got to the point where it can take up to three days to recover from doing two hours of physical work for someone. This is not good, and when we feel like this, we need to completely re-evaluate our life.

If we are suffering due to overwork and burnout, getting back to some sort of healthy balance will not happen overnight. It will need a radical change in the way we think about our work and our health. Yes, we are to do our very best in our work, as doing it unto God (see Colossians 3:23), but God Himself set the precedent to take a day of rest, and has commanded us to do so. When we ignore His design for our life and our health, unfortunately our bodies will bear the consequences of our rebellion.

Bereavement and Grief

"None of us can hold back our spirit from departing. None of us has the power to prevent the day of our death. There is no escaping that obligation, that dark battle." – Ecclesiastes 8:8

"a time to weep and a time to laugh, a time to mourn and a time to dance." – Ecclesiastes 3:4 NIV

The effects of bereavement can be devastating on our body, especially when the death of a loved one is sudden and totally unexpected. Any loss will have a huge impact on us, and will affect our body in one way or another, even if outwardly we look like we are coping. There seems to be a general view that those who are going through grief and bereavement will bounce back from it all after a month or so, and will get back to 'normal life' again fairly quickly. Anyone who has had to take compassionate leave from work may have experienced this from employers and colleagues.

If we have suffered the death of a loved one, we may be able to function in a more or less 'normal' manner after that initial month of mourning, but the physical and emotional effects of our loss can remain with us for a long time and take years to recover from. In some cases, people can be so traumatised by the loss of a loved one that they are actually unable to express any form of emotion at all. If we are already suffering from long-term health problems at the time of suddenly losing a loved one, our body may take much longer to recover from the trauma because it is already in a weakened state.

Let's have a look at some scriptures that show some of the effects on our bodies when we have lost someone close to us.

Following the death of all his loved ones (except his wife), Job expresses the desperate cry of his heart, wishing that he could have died at birth. Many may silently feel like this when faced with the sudden death of their loved ones.

"'Why, then, did you deliver me from my mother's womb? Why didn't you let me die at birth? It would be as though I had never existed, going directly from the womb to the grave." – Job 10:18-19

"My eyes are red with weeping; dark shadows circle my eyes." – Job 16:16

"My eyes are swollen with weeping, and I am but a shadow of my former self." – Job 17:7

King David wished he could have died in place of his son.

"Then the king was deeply moved, and went up to the chamber over the gate, and wept. And as he went, he said thus: "O my son Absalom—my son, my son Absalom—if only I had died in your place! O Absalom my son, my son!" – 2 Samuel 18:33 NKJV

The story of Joseph in Genesis 37:18-35 tells of the time that his brothers deceived their father into believing that Joseph had been killed by wild animals. The scripture below shows the physical effect of grief upon Jacob, under the impression that his son Joseph was dead.

"Then Jacob tore his clothes and dressed himself in burlap. He mourned deeply for his son for a long time. His family all tried to comfort him, but he refused to be comforted. "I will go to my grave mourning for my son," he would say, and then he would weep." – Genesis 37:34-35

Following the very sudden and totally unexpected loss of my father in 2015, a member of my family was struggling to get in touch with her grief in order to express it. She was told by a fellow Christian "not to grieve like those who have no hope". This is taken from the following scripture:

"Now we do not want you to be uninformed, believers, about those who are asleep [in death], so that you will not grieve [for them] as the others do who have no hope [beyond this present life]." – 1 Thessalonians 4:13 AMP

This scripture is entirely true, yet, however well-intentioned the comment from this person may have been, it came across as being used in the wrong way and at the wrong time, leaving my family member questioning herself as to whether she should be grieving at all. It felt to her like a rebuke - like a silent but loaded message that she should not be grieving and crying over the death of a loved one, as this was an indication that she was "acting without hope" - like a non-believer. As Christians, we have to be very careful how we use scripture in delicate situations. At times such as grief, it may be better to love others with practical help, and to comfort them in silence, with a loving arm around their shoulder.

As it says in the following verse:

*"Rejoice with those who rejoice [sharing others' joy], **and weep***

with those who weep [sharing others' grief]." – Romans 12:15 AMP (author's emphasis)

For each of us, the death of a loved one can affect us in ways that we feel incapable of describing. The length of time of our grieving may vary, but God promises to restore us from our place of grief. Let us take comfort in Jesus' promise below:

'Then Jesus said, "Come to me, all of you who are weary and carry heavy burdens, and I will give you rest."' – Matthew 11:28

Whilst the passage below relates to being restored after suffering spiritual attack and persecution, I believe that it can equally apply to God restoring us after a period of grief following the loss of a loved one.

"In his kindness God called you to share in his eternal glory by means of Christ Jesus. So after you have suffered a little while, he will restore, support, and strengthen you, and he will place you on a firm foundation. All power to him forever! Amen." – 1 Peter 5:10-11

At the end, when we ourselves are gathered into God's kingdom, the pain of all that we have lost and mourned will be no more:

"And God will wipe away every tear from their eyes; there shall be no more death, nor sorrow, nor crying. There shall be no more pain..." – Revelation 21:4 NKJV

That final scripture is not just written to comfort us in our grief; it is the word of God, and it is a promise that He will fulfil to all those who believe.

Heavenly Dreams and Visions

Dreams and visions are part of God's means of communicating with us. He communicated in this way with people in both the Old and the New Testament. But receiving dreams and vision are likely to be accompanied by suffering. Yet, many Christians don't believe that we can receive heavenly dreams or visions. They read of these happening in the Bible and think how awesome it is, but they believe that these things have now ceased. I know from personal experience that heavenly dreams and visions do still happen, and they can have an immense effect upon the body – in my own case for a great many months afterwards. You will read more about this in Chapter 6, but for now I will just share that after my encounter, which included spiritual dreams from the Lord, I was so dramatically affected by it that my whole life changed. It left me feeling so weak that I was unable to go out of the house on my own for about six months.

The power of this encounter has never left me; it is a deep part of who I now am, and it dominates the way that I now think, feel and speak. Some Christians think I am a bit 'wacky' when I try to tell them what happened. I don't voluntarily tell people about it; I only share what happened if people ask what I think about dreams and visions. When I had those experiences, the Lord warned me that many people in the Church are now so 'in the world' that they would laugh and scoff if I shared it with them.

Following my first heavenly encounter, I felt a bit like Paul in the following scripture:

"I will reluctantly tell about visions and revelations from the Lord. I was caught up to the third heaven fourteen years ago. Whether I was in my body or out of my body, I don't know—only God knows. Yes, only God knows whether I was in my body or outside my body. But I do know that I was caught up to paradise and heard things so astounding that they cannot be expressed in words, things no human is allowed to tell. That experience is worth boasting about, but I'm not going to do it. I will boast only about my weaknesses. If I wanted to boast, I would be no fool in doing so, because I would be telling the truth. But I won't do it, because I don't want anyone to give me credit beyond what they can see in my life or hear in my message, even though I have received such wonderful revelations from God. So to keep me from becoming proud, I was given a thorn in my flesh, a messenger from Satan to torment me and keep me from becoming proud. Three different times I begged the Lord to take it away. Each time he said, "My grace is all you need. My power works best in weakness." So now I am glad

to boast about my weaknesses, so that the power of Christ can work through me. That's why I take pleasure in my weaknesses, and in the insults, hardships, persecutions, and troubles that I suffer for Christ. For when I am weak, then I am strong." – 2 Corinthians 12:1ᵇ-10

After the heavenly encounter that Paul had, he was given **(by God)**, a 'thorn in the flesh' that tormented him. Like in the story of Job, God permitted a messenger of Satan to come against Paul to torment him in order to keep him from becoming proud. Paul pleaded with God three times to take away this thorn in his flesh, but the Lord said that His grace was all Paul needed in his suffering, and that His power works best in our weakness. In simple language, God said "No" to Paul's begging of Him to take away his suffering because of the heavenly vision he had received.

When people's healings don't happen, maybe those who are part of prayer ministry teams could learn something from the above passage. If you know someone has experienced a heavenly vision, then it's worth pointing out to them that their affliction could be the result of that; in which case, we'll try praying three times, and if they still have the suffering after that, then maybe it is from God to keep them humble. If this is the case, then the most loving and gracious thing that prayer ministers can do is leave the whole matter with God, and simply offer love, understanding and support to the sufferer.

But if you don't know whether someone has experienced a heavenly vision, and they keep coming forward for prayer, perhaps it's worth gently finding out whether or not they've had a vision from God – if they have, then proceed as above. If they haven't, then it's possible that the cause of their suffering is something else (which then needs handling in whichever way is appropriate).

In the Old Testament, Daniel was given dreams and visions by God. In his own words, Daniel describes the impact of these dreams and visions:

*"Then I, Daniel, **was overcome and lay sick for several days.***

*Afterward I got up and performed my duties for the king, but **I was greatly troubled by the vision and could not understand it.**"* – Daniel 8:27

When you read of my encounter in Chapter 6, you will see that I was ill afterwards; I could not understand what God was revealing to me either, and I was deeply troubled by it for two years. But then suddenly, God invaded my life in October 2011, with the interpretation so that I could understand it, and He has been revealing things ever since.

Concerning his sufferings and the dreams and visions God gave him, Job vividly described the effect these had upon him:

*"I think, 'My bed will comfort me, and sleep will ease my misery,' but then **you shatter me with dreams and terrify me with visions.** I would rather be strangled— rather die than suffer like this."* – Job 7:13-15 (author's emphasis)

Job's friend Elihu says,

*"For God speaks again and again, though people do not recognize it. **He speaks in dreams, in visions of the night, when deep sleep falls on people as they lie in their beds. He whispers in their ears and terrifies them with warnings.**"* – Job 33:14-16 (author's emphasis)

To conclude this section, I would like to encourage you to read a book by Darren Hibbs, titled *The Year of the Lord's Favor – A Prophetic Message to America.* This man had a powerful heavenly encounter a few days before the catastrophic event that occurred in America in 2001; a day that surely must be etched in people's minds forever: the destruction of the Twin Towers on 9/11. His story will shake you to the core and will leave a deep impact in you, hopefully forever changing the way you think regarding the subject of dreams and visions from the Lord. I have included his book in the Recommended Reading section at the back.

Those who have had dreams and visions from God don't usually talk about them in order to boast about their experience, but to warn people of what God has shown them. This is usually a very serious matter and is not an easy thing to do, as mocking and ridicule are often the result of trying to alert others to heed God's warnings. But God seems to be increasingly giving His children dreams and visons, and for very good reasons - to wake up His Church from spiritual deception and complacency caused by the daily lures and temptations of living in this fallen world. It is as if this is God's last-ditch attempt to wake up the Church... before He decides that 'time is up', and then pours out His long-held-back wrath upon this earth, upon unbelievers **and** the lukewarm, watered-down, compromising, and unrepentant churches that exist today.

Chapter 5

Lack of Faith, Unbelief, and Unrepentant Sin

Part 2

Let's now have a look at the suffering we can experience in our lives and in our bodies because of these things.

Lack of Faith and Unbelief

It is difficult to say whether lack of faith and unbelief are one and the same thing. Many may think that they are the same, but I personally think there is a difference. I would say that a lack of faith in an area of our life as a Christian does not mean that we have no faith at all for something that we are praying for, but rather that we have what Jesus describes as 'little faith'; whereas unbelief is a very definite statement that we have no belief for it.

Below are a few scriptures relating to having lack of faith/little faith, and following those, I will then list some verses to do with unbelief.

a) Lack of faith/little faith

"And if God cares so wonderfully for wildflowers that are here

today and thrown into the fire tomorrow, he will certainly care for you. **Why do you have so little faith?***"* – Matthew 6:30 (author's emphasis)

'The disciples went and woke him up, shouting, "Lord, save us! We're going to drown!" Jesus responded, "Why are you afraid? **You have so little faith!***" Then he got up and rebuked the wind and waves, and suddenly there was a great calm. The disciples were amazed. "Who is this man?" they asked. "Even the winds and waves obey him!"'* – Matthew 8:25-27 (author's emphasis)

"Then Peter called to him, "Lord, if it's really you, tell me to come to you, walking on the water." "Yes, come," Jesus said. So Peter went over the side of the boat and walked on the water toward Jesus. But when he saw the strong wind and the waves, he was terrified and began to sink. "Save me, Lord!" he shouted. Jesus immediately reached out and grabbed him. **"You have so little faith,"** *Jesus said. "Why did you doubt me?" When they climbed back into the boat, the wind stopped."* – Matthew 14:28-32 (author's emphasis)

"At this they began to argue with each other because they hadn't brought any bread. Jesus knew what they were saying, so he said, **"You have so little faith!** *Why are you arguing with each other about having no bread? Don't you understand even yet? Don't you remember the 5,000 I fed with five loaves, and the baskets of leftovers you picked up?"* – Matthew 16:7-9 (author's emphasis)

b) Unbelief

"He returned to Nazareth, his hometown. When he taught there in the synagogue, everyone was amazed and said, "Where does he get this wisdom and the power to do miracles?" Then they scoffed, "He's just the carpenter's son, and we know Mary, his mother, and his brothers—James, Joseph, Simon, and Judas. All his sisters live right here among us. Where did he learn all these things?" And they were deeply offended and refused to believe in him. Then Jesus told them, "A prophet is honored everywhere except in his own hometown and

*among his own family." **And so he did only a few miracles there because of their unbelief."** – Matthew 13:54-58 (author's emphasis)*

*"Then Jesus told them, "A prophet is honored everywhere except in his own hometown and among his relatives and his own family." And **because of their unbelief,** he couldn't do any miracles among them except to place his hands on a few sick people and heal them. And he was amazed at their unbelief." – Mark 6:4-6 (author's emphasis)*

*"After Jesus rose from the dead early on Sunday morning, the first person who saw him was Mary Magdalene, the woman from whom he had cast out seven demons. She went to the disciples, who were grieving and weeping, and told them what had happened. But when she told them that Jesus was alive and she had seen him, they didn't believe her. Afterward he appeared in a different form to two of his followers who were walking from Jerusalem into the country. They rushed back to tell the others, but no one believed them. Still later he appeared to the eleven disciples as they were eating together. He rebuked them **for their stubborn unbelief** because they refused to believe those who had seen him after he had been raised from the dead." – Mark 16:9-14 (author's emphasis)*

I would suggest that having little faith or lacking in faith to some degree may result in us experiencing suffering and not receiving what we are praying for, maybe because we keep tossing to-and-fro between believing and then having less faith for it due to some circumstances. But with being in a state of unbelief, we are not even asking God to do something for us, let alone expecting Him to do something miraculous. The above passages of scripture do show the difference. In the case of lack of faith/little faith, Jesus could clearly see that in each situation there was a measure of faith in existence. But in the case of unbelief, He saw nothing but offense and rejection towards the miracles that He did; even the miracle of God raising Him from the dead.

In my own life, many times I have heard people in the Church say things like, "You just need more faith for your healing". This is interesting because Jesus says that we only need faith the size of a mustard seed! (see Matthew 17:20). Well, for my own part, I do have faith that is at least the size of a mustard seed, if not the size of a mountain, yet I cannot personally make my healing happen.

One lady told me, after only a few minutes of me talking to her, that I had a 'spirit of unbelief', yet I explained to her that this could not be the case as the Lord had healed me of many things, and also things that I had prayed for others. If I had unbelief, then it meant that I had no belief whatsoever that God could heal, and as such the Lord would not have done those miraculous healings in answer to my prayers. She didn't respond, but turned and walked away.

The Lord knows that my heart's desire is to be healed fully of every ailment and condition that has been a part of my life for so long. Because the healing has not yet manifest, it does not mean that I lack faith, or have little faith, or have no faith at all for it. I have left it in God's hands to take care of. I cannot keep going back to it and taking it out of His hands simply because of impatience. That would definitely be showing a sign of lack of faith or unbelief in Him.

I believe that it takes more faith to give something over to God and to leave it there, trusting in Him to do whatever is His will for it, and quenching every desire in ourselves to take it back off Him. To me, that is **enormous** faith, not a lack of it.

Unconfessed and Unrepentant Sin in our Lives

The very nature of this category means that this section will be quite long, but I feel that such an issue warrants it. It is a subject that many in the Church now seem to want to ignore, but God will not overlook it. He has called us to repent of our sins, not just when we gave our lives to Christ, but also as we live each day of our lives in Christ. We are not perfect, and as such, we will think, say or do sinful things each day. God wants us to have humble hearts and confess and repent of them, and receive His forgiveness and cleansing each time we mess up.

In this section, we will look at the suffering that we can experience as a result of sin. A thorough search of the Bible will reveal many scriptures that give evidence of the consequential physical effects of **unrepentant** sin in our bodies. We are talking about all sin, not just sexual sin. So, let's have a look at a list of sins; quite a few of these being things that many of us would not even consider as being sinful. When we accept God's word as being right and holy, the 'big sins' are obvious, and with which we ought to have no doubt, although rather disturbingly many in the Church in recent years are now beginning to have differing views on some of the aspects of the 'big' sins listed below.

The 'Big' Sins

Murder: Taking away another person's life. To my understanding, this also includes taking our own life. As difficult as it can be to comprehend, suicide is the taking of our life before God's appointed time for us to die. As I mentioned in Chapter 1, I have suffered with suicidal thoughts, so if you are struggling with thoughts of suicide, I would encourage you to talk to someone you know and trust so they can help you. God values you and has great plans for your life.

Even though it is now legalised, another sensitive subject that is hotly debated today is abortion; the killing of the life of unborn babies in the womb. A baby is a separate, living human being inside the mother, with its own DNA and may even have a different blood group than its mother. The creation of human life in the womb is a miracle of God, regardless of the circumstances that surrounded the conception. The baby should not be punished for its creation simply because the mother's circumstances may be unfavourable. Having the baby and then placing the child in the care of loving adoptive parents would be a gift of life to the baby, and would be an honourable thing to do before God.

If you have had an abortion and are suffering physically,

emotionally and mentally because of this decision, I encourage you to come before God in repentance. He will embrace you with His mercy, grace and love, and will forgive you, and give you a fresh start.

Another area that I feel should be included in this category is the issue of euthanasia. There are many debates about this, but in some countries, this practice is now legal. People from countries where it is not legal are travelling to countries where it is, so that they can put an end to their suffering. It is such a delicate subject because it is to do with long-term pain and suffering, but again, euthanasia is the choice to end life ahead of God's appointed time.

Theft: Burglary, robbery, muggings, petty theft, shoplifting, taking things from your place of work for your own personal use without your employer's permission.

Sexual Sin: Homosexuality, lesbianism and the wide variety of sexual orientations that have become part of the culture of this world in recent years; rape, sexual abuse, molestation, incest, adultery, fornication, lust, masturbation, pornography, paedophilia, bestiality, and any other form of sexual perversion.

Violence: Civil commotion and riots, gang violence, domestic abuse, child abuse, emotional and verbal abuse, bullying in all situations, forceful mistreatment of vulnerable people, and mistreatment of animals/pets.

Fraud: Any criminal activity used to deceive and defraud others for the purpose of personal, monetary or property gain, whether in business or in personal circumstances.

I may have missed some examples above, but feel free to add any that come to mind.

Now let's look at the long list of 'less obvious' sins, which are the sort that we tend to easily overlook and excuse. Perhaps we would call them 'character flaws' which we say we can't help doing or that's just the way we are. We often expect others to accept and live with these behaviours of ours, yet we resist making much effort to repent of them and change our ways. But interestingly, we don't tolerate similar sins in other people! The way we can know whether our habits are sins is to ask ourselves if Jesus would do them.

'Less Obvious' Sins

Anger: Hatred, bitterness, resentment, strife, hostility, holding grudges, verbal outbursts, unforgiveness (any of these toward others, God, ourselves, or circumstances), all of which we do not process and allow to build up. However, there is a place for righteous anger/indignation, to stand up against ungodliness and evil.

Control and manipulation: including bullying, intimidation, domination, oppression, perfectionism.

Coveting: Desiring things that belong to other people.

Disillusionment/Discontentment: About any aspect of life, jobs, money, possessions, relationships. This is a difficult area because there can be many times when life hits us hard, causing us to feel disillusioned or discontented with our circumstances, and we seem unable to focus on God in the middle of it all. When we lose sight of God, Satan is able to play havoc with our thoughts, causing us to fall into a spiral of despair about our life, and making us believe that things will never change. He convinces us that God has abandoned us and that there is no point in us asking Him to help us. We then believe Satan's lies and can end up in a vicious cycle.

I would suggest that these things only become a sin when we give up and stay in this cycle, and don't have any motivation to do anything to change the situation; where it affects areas of our life such as our performance at work, or not being attentive in our relationships. When we feel that there is no way out, the only way that we will be able to see the light at the end of the tunnel is by surrendering it all to God, asking Him to help us see the situation as He sees it, discovering what He is teaching us in it, and helping us respond to our circumstances as Jesus would.

Envy: Including jealousy and competitiveness.

Idolatry: Putting anything else over and above God and focusing on it or pursuing it obsessively; e.g., sports, sports stars, celebrities, soap operas and other TV programmes, cars, possessions, money, homes, jobs, the latest gadgets, mobile phones, social media, our looks, and even idolising our spouse or our children.

Lack of Self-Control: Emotional outbursts that are uncontrolled; physical and verbal abuse; anger; overeating; excessive drinking; partying; overspending; acquiring possessions; excessive TV usage and programme choice; computer usage and website choices; choice of books, magazines, and music; untidiness; secret lust and fantasy; other secret thoughts and imaginations.

Pride: Boasting, puffing ourselves up, superiority, self-righteousness, stubbornness, independence (the self-made man attitude), unteachable attitude.

Selfishness/Self-centeredness and other attitudes: Demanding that our needs and wishes be met above everything else, selfish with our time and money, being inconsiderate and thoughtless of others, discourteous, lack of respect for others, impatience, annoyance, irritability (toward others, ourselves, external situations beyond our control, and even toward God), self-pity, indifference, aloofness, cynicism, callousness, coldness, hard-heartedness, taking offence.

Serious Addictions: Drugs, alcohol, smoking, sex, gambling.

Sins of our words: Gossip, foul language, harsh words, coarse joking, jesting (making fun of others), belittling and intimidating words, insults and slander, deception, denial, pretence, lying/bearing false witness, blasphemy/profanity, corrupting talk, sarcasm, unwarranted criticism, judgmentalism (assuming a situation and making a personal judgment about it based on inadequate/minimal information).

Subtle Addictions: Horoscopes; the following **in excess:** shopping, food, computer games, TV, mobile phone usage, Internet chat rooms, social media.

Ungodliness: Living our life with no thought or regard for God whatsoever. Our lives display this through our words, our attitudes, and our actions.

Ungratefulness: Lack of showing or expressing our thanks and appreciation to others; grumbling, complaining unnecessarily, moaning, "glass half empty" outlook.

Vainglory: Doing the right things but with the wrong motive; i.e., doing good deeds because we want to be noticed and so that others will thank us and praise us.

Worldliness: Lust for more (possessions, money, promotions, etc.); inappropriate dress to get ourselves noticed by others; inappropriate behaviour to draw attention; going along with and following the practices of society around us and peer pressure in order to fit in and feel accepted and valued, even when we know that what we are succumbing to is unbiblical.

Worry/fear: Including anxiety, frustration, apprehension. This is a delicate area because many people suffer from anxiety as a medical condition and may require treatment with medication and therapy. As I mentioned in Chapter 1, I have suffered with symptoms related to fear and anxiety, causing me to have a breakdown which needed treatment with medication, so I understand how difficult this is. The reason I have listed this is because God's word instructs us not to have a spirit of fear (see Romans 8:15 & 2 Timothy 1:7), as this is the opposite of having faith and trust in God. This takes us back to the section above concerning lack of faith or unbelief. The Lord knows that being fearful, anxious or worrying are not good for us, and so He exhorts us to pray to Him and receive His peace.

"Don't worry about anything; instead, pray about everything. Tell God what you need, and thank him for all he has done. Then you will

experience God's peace, which exceeds anything we can understand. His peace will guard your hearts and minds as you live in Christ Jesus." – Philippians 4:6-7

Now we come to a category which Christians really ought to know are sinful, but shockingly there is now a huge rise in spiritual deception in Christianity, which is accepting, embracing and promoting many of the practices listed below:

Other Spiritual Experiences: Witchcraft; Satanism; the occult; New Age and other alternative spiritualism; consulting mediums, clairvoyants; dowsing; crystals; orbs; Ouija boards; other séance activities; alternative healing where faith in God/Jesus is absent; contacting the spirits of the dead; ghost-hunting; hypnosis and hypnotherapy or anything involving mind control; divining; Eastern mystic spiritualism; any faith or religion that denies God **and** His Son Jesus Christ as the Messiah and our Lord and Saviour; worship and obsession of angels; Freemasonry and other associated/affiliated organizations; palm reading; fortune telling; tarot cards; tea-leaf reading; horoscopes; astrology; yoga; levitation; channelling; scientology; any cults, even so-called Christian cults.

The above lists may look extensive, but again, I am sure that I will have missed some examples of less obvious sins. Please feel free to add any that spring to your mind.

Now let's look at some passages of scripture on the subject of sin, and **the suffering** we can experience in our bodies when we are unrepentant. We will see that these scriptures are clear, and that they do not need any intellectual interpretation or clarification. **All** sin has consequences, and many of the consequences will affect our bodies, both physically and emotionally, as well as affect the validity of our faith when we are in public.

"When I refused to confess my sin, my body wasted away, and I groaned all day long. Day and night your hand of discipline was heavy on me. My strength evaporated like water in the summer heat." – Psalm 32:3-4 (author's emphasis)

114

"For I do confess my guilt and iniquity; ***I am filled with anxiety because of my sin.*** *"* – Psalm 38:18 AMP (author's emphasis)

*"**Before I was afflicted I went astray,** but now I keep and honor Your word [with loving obedience]."* – Psalm 119: 67 AMP (author's emphasis)

"Don't be impressed with your own wisdom. ***Instead, fear the LORD and turn away from evil. Then you will have healing for your body and strength for your bones.*** *"* – Proverbs 3:7-8 (author's emphasis)

"A peaceful heart leads to a healthy body; ***jealousy is like cancer in the bones.*** *"* – Proverbs 14:30 (author's emphasis)

"Jesus answered, "I assure you and most solemnly say to you, ***everyone who practices sin habitually is a slave of sin.*** *"* – John 8:34 AMP (author's emphasis)

"Let no one deceive you with empty arguments [that encourage you to sin], for because of these things ***the wrath of God comes upon the sons of disobedience [those who habitually sin].*** *"* – Ephesians 5:6 AMP (author's emphasis)

With regard to the most prominent sin that is visible in the world and the Church today, the following passage is very clear concerning its effects:

*"**Run from sexual sin! No other sin so clearly affects the body as this one does. For sexual immorality is a sin against your own body.** Don't you realize that your body is the temple of the Holy Spirit, who lives in you and was given to you by God? You do not belong to yourself, for God bought you with a high price.* ***So you must honor God with your body.*** *"* – 1 Corinthians 6:18-20 (author's emphasis)

Paul states categorically and without any ambiguity (that we have no need to interpret his words to mean anything other than what is stated) that **sexual sin** has the **worst affect upon our bodies**, worse than any other type of sin mentioned throughout the entirety of the Bible. As we see in the passage below, it is God's will that we stay away from **all** sexual sin and to live holy lives, controlling our own bodies. This must surely be for our good! This being the case, why do we think that God will accept our desire and decision to live our lives in ways that are contrary to this? And why do we think that our rebellion to His word will not have any consequences in our lives, especially in our bodies?

"Finally, dear brothers and sisters, we urge you in the name of the Lord Jesus to live in a way that pleases God, as we have taught you... For you remember what we taught you by the authority of the Lord Jesus. God's will is for you to be holy, so stay away from all sexual sin. Then each of you will control his own body and live in holiness and honor — not in lustful passion like the pagans who do not know God and his ways." – 1 Thessalonians 4:1ᵃ, & vs 2-5

In relation to any suffering that we may have in our bodies due to our past sins, many in the Church believe that once we have given our lives to Christ, all our physical illnesses are healed. I would just like to clarify something here: Scripture is clear that Jesus' death on the cross and His shed blood has brought about the remission of all **the sins** of our **past** life, as shown in the verse below:

*"Him God hath set forth to be a propitiation through faith in His blood, to declare His righteousness for the remission of **sins that are past**, ..."* – Romans 3:25 KJ21 (author's emphasis)

However, it **may not** be the case that we are healed of the physical consequences of those past sins. God is the only One who can make the decision on this. He may well choose to do this in a person's life, but equally He may choose to leave us with the scars of our past sins, even though our involvement in those past sins has been forgiven. The reality needs to be faced that complete physical healing of all our ailments, at the very moment of becoming born again and filled with the Holy Spirit, is not something that we can categorically guarantee will be fulfilled by God without exception. It would be lovely if this was the case, but often the scars of our past sins can remain with us, keeping us humble before God and surrendered to Him. Still having the scars – the physical consequences of our past sins – is enough to keep us from ever desiring to go back to our old ways of life. Carrying the suffering of what our scars represent will enable us to come to Jesus in our weakness and receive His strength.

If God **does** heal us of all the years of damage that our sins have done to our bodies, it is a wonderful thing. However, a word of warning: referring to the incident recorded in John 5:1-15, where Jesus healed a man who had been lame for 38 years because of his life of sin; after Jesus had healed him, He then **warned** him, saying:

*"Now you are well; so **stop sinning, or something even worse may happen to you.**"* – John 5:14ᵇ (author's emphasis)

Have we got the message in this verse? This man had been unable to walk for 38 years; a devastating consequence of his sins. Jesus mercifully heals him, but then He warns him that if he **carries on sinning**, something **worse** than the lifetime of lameness he had already endured could come upon him!

So, it is clear from these words of Jesus that if we have received a healing but then fall back into the sins that we were previously involved in, it is very possible that we could end up with worse physical problems than the ones Jesus healed us of.

Peter also confirms this:

*"And when people escape from the wickedness of the world by knowing our Lord and Savior Jesus Christ **and then get tangled up and enslaved by sin again, they are worse off than before.**"* – 2 Peter 2:20 (author's emphasis)

If Jesus has healed us of something, yet we continue to sin and then get sick again, why should we expect Him to heal us again? Yes, He could do so, but our disobedience to His command to stop sinning **after** He has healed us of something is the equivalent of spitting in the face of His gracious mercy, love and forgiveness, and as the writer to the Hebrews puts it:

"If we deliberately keep on sinning after we have received the knowledge of the truth, no sacrifice for sins is left, but only a fearful expectation of judgment and of raging fire that will consume the enemies of God. Anyone who rejected the law of Moses died without mercy on the testimony of two or three witnesses. **How much more severely do you think someone deserves to be punished who has trampled the Son of God underfoot, who has treated as an unholy thing the blood of the covenant that sanctified them, and who has insulted the Spirit of grace?** *For we know him who said, "It is mine to avenge; I will repay," and again, "The Lord will judge his people." It is a dreadful thing to fall into the hands of the living God."* – Hebrews 10:26-31 NIV (author's emphasis)

This is such a sobering passage from God's word, and sadly it is something that much of the Church today is failing to preach.

Jesus' warning of something worse coming upon us is not a threat; it is a statement of fact. Jesus knows what sin can and will do to our bodies if we keep returning to the ways of our flesh. His stern words to the lame man whom He healed was actually a mark of His deep love for him, exhorting him to stay away from sin because of the physical consequences that could ensue.

Ryle has this to say on this matter:

"We are taught the lesson that recovery from sickness ought to impress upon us. That lesson is contained in the solemn words which our Saviour addressed to the man he had cured; 'Sin no more, lest a worse thing come upon thee.' Every sickness and sorrow is the voice of God speaking to us. Each has its peculiar message. Happy are they who have an eye to see God's hand and an ear to hear his voice in all that happens to them. Nothing in this world happens by chance. And as it is with sickness, so it is with recovery. Renewed health should send us back to our post in the world with a deeper hatred of sin, a more thorough watchfulness over our own ways and a more constant purpose of mind to live to God. Far too often the excitement

and novelty of returning to health tempt us to forget the vows and intentions of the sick-room. There are spiritual dangers attending a recovery! Well would it be for us all after illness to grave these words on our hearts; 'Let me sin no more, lest a worse thing come upon me.'" [3]

Yet, despite the warnings in scripture, sin **within** the Church is escalating at an alarming rate, and it has now got past the point where it is merely tolerated. Openly in the media, and on quite a regular basis, we see examples of many church denominations now proudly accepting, embracing and celebrating the practices of those who remain unrepentant, and even appointing them into positions of church leadership. Many churches today seem to be in quite serious rebellion against the word of God. As we will see in the passage below addressed to the Church at Thyatira, Jesus gives a severe warning about how He will deal with the Church that teaches its flock to commit sexual sin. This warning from the Lord should speak loud and clear to the **whole** Church today:

"But I have this complaint against you. You are permitting that woman—that Jezebel who calls herself a prophet—to lead my servants astray. She teaches them to commit sexual sin and to eat food offered to idols. I gave her time to repent, but she does not want to turn away from her immorality. "Therefore, I will throw her on a bed of suffering, and those who commit adultery with her will suffer greatly unless they repent and turn away from her evil deeds." – Revelation 2:20-22

Whatever position we hold in the Church, or if we are simply part of the congregation, if we are involved in sexual sin, it is clear that we will experience suffering. Our only solution is to repent and obey God's word.

Finally, a very powerful passage of scripture concerning our suffering physically for Christ, and what the purpose of our suffering is ultimately for: **to be 'finished with sin'.**

"So then, since Christ suffered physical pain, you must arm yourselves with the same attitude he had, and be ready to suffer, too.

For if you have suffered physically for Christ, you have finished with sin. You won't spend the rest of your lives chasing your own desires, but you will be anxious to do the will of God. You have had enough in the past of the evil things that godless people enjoy..." – 1 Peter 4:1-3 (author's emphasis)

In effect, we should live our lives in such a way that we are not going through suffering **because** of sin in our life, but that our suffering has got us to the place where we are now so **sick of sin** that we are **finished with it.** This takes us right back to the purpose of all suffering that is stated in the scripture passage below:

*"For we know that all creation has been groaning as in the pains of childbirth right up to the present time. **And we believers also groan,** even though we have the Holy Spirit within us as a foretaste of future glory, for **we long for our bodies to be released from sin and suffering. We, too, wait with eager hope for the day when God will give us our full rights as his adopted children, including the new bodies he has promised us."* – Romans 8:22-23 (author's emphasis)

In closing, let us repent and be doing all that we can to ensure that **we are suffering for doing what is right** for God's kingdom (see 1 Peter 3:14 & 1 Peter 4:19), rather than suffering as a consequence of disobedience to His word and unrepentant sin.

Closing this chapter (Parts 1 and 2)

This chapter has been a long journey of discovery concerning the many reasons that we may experience suffering in our lives. Before we pre-judge someone's situation, let us seek God for wisdom and discernment and find out whether the reasons for their suffering is for spiritual and godly reasons, rather than assume that it is because of a lack of faith, unbelief, or unrepentant sin. But if it is because of these things, then let us lovingly show them God's word to help them repent and receive His forgiveness.

A person's life of suffering could be for any of the reasons mentioned in this chapter, including by the permissive will of God. If we don't take the time to hear the person's story, then we cannot possibly know what the circumstances are that have caused them to be in suffering. Having an assumption of what we think is wrong, and trying to fix the person based on our assumptions without hearing their story, is something that Jesus points out below:

"Why do you focus on the flaw in someone else's life and fail to notice the glaring flaws of your own life? How could you say to your friend, 'Here, let me show you where you're wrong,' when you are guilty of even more than he is? You are overly critical, splitting hairs and being a hypocrite! You must acknowledge your own blind spots and deal with them before you will be able to deal with the blind spot of your friend." — Luke 6:41-42 TPT

Let us not be of this kind of spirit. Let us do all that we can to remain true to God's word by speaking the truth in love to guide and correct into right living where it is needed, and to show love, understanding, empathy, grace and support to all who continue to suffer even after many years of prayer for healing.

Chapter 6

When Healing Doesn't Happen – God's Purpose in the Pain

"I cry out to God Most High, to God who
will fulfill his purpose for me."
Psalm 57:2

In this chapter I would like to share with you the story of God's purpose in the pain; in the journey He has taken me through since I gave my life to Christ, and which He is still taking me through to this day. Whilst it is the last chapter in this book, it is by no means the end of my story. It is a story that will continue until I draw my last breath, or until the Lord returns…whichever comes first!

We pick the story up where we left it at the end of Chapter 2 – the troubling mystery of when healing doesn't happen. Any suffering or pain, short or long-term, can certainly feel like God is nowhere in sight, and that He has left us to fend for ourselves, in our wilderness of suffering. When God doesn't seem to be doing something for us, particularly in the area of being healed of our suffering, this mystery is to do with what is His sovereign will and what is His permissive will. His sovereign will is that, yes it is His will to heal. Healing is part of the nature of who God is. However,

His permissive will is what He permits to happen to us in our lives, which He wants to use for His purposes and for His glory. Such times can be short, or they can be very long. The duration is only known by God, and He doesn't seem to let us in on His timescale.

So, let's ask ourselves what seems to be an almost unanswerable question:

"What do we do when healing doesn't happen?"

Wanting so much to be healed is a deep and powerful longing, and when it doesn't happen, it has the potential to bring us to despair and even cause us to lose our faith and give up on God altogether. I will admit to you that I have felt this on many occasions. But in those desperate times, the one thing that has gripped me is the deep yearning in my soul to be with the Lord forever, and not be found to have forsaken Him, and be left outside the gates as a castaway. This longing has caused me to know that, despite my suffering, God has a plan for my life and that each day of my life is part of His plan. In my suffering, I have learned that God wants to take me on a journey of discovery of all that He wants to accomplish in my life for His purposes.

In your own suffering, I believe that God has a plan and a journey for you too; a journey that may surprise you and lead you into areas of work for Him that you have no knowledge of or even ability to do in your own natural strength.

I had no idea what God had in store for me in my suffering, but I would now like to share it with you, to encourage you that God **really does** have a purpose for you in your pain. He can reveal to you the 'treasure in the trash' and make 'a message out of the mess'.

The following is the story of the path God took me on, when my healing didn't happen. Each time I reflect upon it, and every day that I walk through this journey of suffering, the reality of God's presence in my life, and the mind-blowing things He has brought about in my life of pain, brings me to tears. In my own feeble self, I could not have achieved any of what I am about to share with you. It is **all** God's doing, and it is most certainly all for His glory...

Ranting at God

When I first gave my life to Christ, my initial reaction to not being healed of any of my long-term physical ailments was to get frustrated and sulk! I then got a bit angry at God and said, "What sort of God are you if you say that you can heal people, but you are going to leave me like this? Why do you heal some things in me but then leave me with all the ailments that have plagued me for most of my life? Why can you not just heal the whole lot and let me live the rest of my life free from this unrelenting pain and exhaustion? I am sure that I would be a much better witness for you if I was fully healed."

To most of my rantings like this, the Lord remained silent. This did not help how I felt! But somehow, I found the strength to grit my teeth and get through each day. At this point, I was a full-time mother at home, so I was able to find time to shut myself off in my bedroom and pray and read my Bible whilst my baby was asleep in her cot. Later, when she went to school, I was able to have even more time to myself to seek the Lord. During these times of unrelenting health problems, it caused me to seek the Lord even harder. In my times of isolation, I found that the Lord would speak things to me, just like He did at the Good Friday service. I began to write down all the things He spoke to me, and His words sustained me through the many years of isolation I had to endure.

God's Purpose Begins

It then began to dawn on me that God had got me alone so that He could speak words to rebuke me, correct me, cleanse me, and forgive me. He was permitting these long-term health issues to draw me to Him so that I would seek Him much more than I would if I was fully healthy. On days when my pain is much less, I have a tendency to fill up all my time with doing anything except seeking the Lord or spending any time with Him. It seems to me that the only way I ever do have this deeper relationship with the Lord is when I am in pain and suffering. It throws me at His feet in prayer because I feel so weak that I literally can't do much else.

As the years went by, with no healing in sight for my long-term conditions, I reflected on my life as one who professes to be a follower of Christ, and the awful reality overwhelmed me that I had **not** been faithful to Him in obeying His word. Even though the Lord would speak things into my soul in very powerful ways, in my actual daily life I was a compromising, half-hearted, lukewarm believer, with my focus very much on the things of this world. As a result of this, having my heart set on Jesus and making sure I was living my life in obedience to His word was not even on my radar. I knew something needed to change in me, but I didn't know what to do or how to do it. I desperately wanted to know what God required me to do to break free from my life of sin, but nothing seemed to change.

One Door Closes – A New Door Opens

After the breakup of my first marriage, in 2006 I married Chris. One morning, whilst we were on our honeymoon, I was quietly and peacefully praying alone in our holiday cottage, asking the Lord to show me what my future Christian life might look like, seeing as I had made such a mess of it up to that point. As I sat there silently waiting on the Lord, and reading a devotional book by Frances J. Roberts, all of a sudden, the incredible power of the Spirit of God leapt off the pages and thundered into my being like a lightning bolt. This time the awesome power caused my body to literally jump up off the bed! Once gain, my heart began pounding from this sudden invasion into my time of quiet solitude. The words that I read, which I equally heard deep in my being, made me weep for days.

There I was, on honeymoon, just days after making my wedding vows to my new husband, yet the Lord chose this moment to speak words to me about my lukewarm, complacent, half-hearted relationship with Him, exhorting me to **renew my vows to Him.** Here are the words that impacted my soul, and have remained rooted in the depths of my being ever since:

"Renew your vows, and I will revive your ministry. There is a life ahead for you into which you could not have entered before. There is a work ready for you, and I have prepared you for it. It is too wonderful to miss. It will be silent but powerful... You will serve me in ways you have never heard of before. It is My work. I have laid it out for you. Keep clear of man's work. Stay free to do Mine. You will not miss it if you keep close to Me and stay sensitive to My Spirit." [1]

I knew this was the Lord speaking. I didn't know what His words meant, but I knew in the very depths of me that the words He was speaking to me would be fulfilled. Yet I didn't have a clue what this would look like or how it would happen.

A 'Wake Up' Call!

Three years went by, with me still dragging myself through my days of ill-health and isolation, when again I heard a voice speak to me in the same manner as the previous times. The words hit me like an arrow in my soul, and shook me to the core.

The words I heard were, **"WAKE UP, CHURCH!"**

My heart started pounding so hard, I thought it would burst out of my chest. A sense of reverential fear and trembling came upon me, and an acute sense of God's holiness, righteousness and justice filled my whole being. I felt a heavy burden, and a sense of foreboding come upon me that I could not shake off. It was quite frightening, since I didn't know what it was about.

I felt a deep compelling inside me that these words from the Lord were a command from Him to write a book...about waking up the Church. My first utterly stunned reaction to this was, "WHAT? You have got to be joking Lord! I am okay at writing a shopping list, but a book? Are you serious?!" In spite of my protestations, I could not dismiss what I heard and felt in my spirit. Yet the whole thing made no sense to me at all. I was a housewife and a mother, not an author! I had absolutely no idea what the Lord wanted to wake His Church up about, let alone know how to go about writing a book, and certainly not one on such a serious matter. The thought of all this terrified me. I hoped that I was just imagining it all, but the more I tried to fight against the words, the more intense they became. At times it felt like all of the heavenly host were yelling at me because there seemed to be no let-up in the frequency of these powerful words, which were relentlessly reverberating inside of me, like a nonstop echo.

When I had lost all my will to fight against this invasion into my life, I finally yielded to God's will and said that I would do what He asked. I decided that the only thing I could do to get a measure of peace again was to rest in the knowledge that if God wanted something done, then He would reveal it to me at some point. I did have a deep sense that it would be a serious and urgent message, so I was not going to attempt to write one single word without His specific instruction. So, I waited…and waited.

Another two years went by. The peace that I had hoped for, in agreeing to do God's will, eluded me. I got so fed up with these words going around in my head that the only way I could get it all out of my mind was to fill up my daily life with endless hours of gardening and decorating… yes, even though I felt so unwell and exhausted all the time! I was basically trying to block God out of my life each day, and I wouldn't allow Him any room to speak to me with His words to wake up the Church. I'd had enough of waiting. I decided that I no longer wanted to hear what God wanted to say, and I convinced myself again that it was all just in my imagination.

My goodness, how wrong could I have been!

A Strange Affliction

In October 2011, an incident occurred where the Lord revealed to me very clearly the critical thing that was missing in my life as a believer caught in the trap of repetitive sinful behaviour. The things He revealed to me in that agonising time were to become the message of the book to wake up the Church. I had desperately sought the Lord for the answer since 1994, but for the Lord's **own** reasons and His own purposes, He chose to make me wait for seventeen years for the answer.

When God wants to get your attention, He doesn't mess about! One day, whilst I was up a ladder painting a wall, deeply engrossed in endless hours of decorating, trying to block out God, He must have decided that He had had enough of my rebellion because, when I had finished the last bit of painting and had got to the bottom of the ladder, the Lord broke through my resistance in a powerful way, causing me to collapse on the floor, and bringing my life to a sudden halt. A strange affliction came upon me in an instant, and I can only describe this as something that was brought into my life through a supernatural experience, as there are no words in my vocabulary that are adequate to express what occurred. Yes, this supernatural encounter brought **another** affliction, to add on top of the physical suffering that I had been carrying for most of my life. I thought I had previously been in immense pain, but what now came upon me by the hand of the Lord was a level of pain that I cannot describe, coupled with severe distress and terror. A raging fire seemed to burn within my body causing sweat to pour out of me almost nonstop for two weeks, yet I did not have a fever that would have caused this to happen.

I felt very ill and very weak, and had no ability to think or speak in a coherent manner, but I had an intense desire to read my Bible. My head was immersed in it from morning to night. What the Lord was causing me to read was what He wanted to reveal to me about my own sinful life as a believer, and also to write in the book to wake up the Church. The message He wanted to reveal was 'sin **within** the Church, and what Jesus had to say about it'.

What I was shown to write was what Jesus had to say **to me personally** about my own compromising, complacent attitude towards His holy word, and the repetitive, unconfessed and unrepentant sin within my own life, as a professing follower of Christ. It was a gruelling experience, but it was absolutely essential. God had to show me personally what His message was about in relation to my own life, before He could equip me and enable me to write His book about waking up the Church.

Despite the weakness that overwhelmed me, I somehow managed to pick up a pen and a notebook and I began to write, even though I didn't know what was going to come out of the end of the pen onto the paper. I simply asked the Lord to cause me to write what **He** wanted the Church to hear. Having waited for over two years to know what it was that the Lord wanted to wake His Church up about, miraculously by the power of the Holy Spirit, in that two-week period, I had completed the manuscript and the book was published in 2013. The title of the book is, *'Come on Church! Wake Up! Sin Within the Church and What Jesus Has to Say About It'.*

The Lord planted the seed of that book in 2009, and He fulfilled it in 2013. Despite all my frustration and my trying to 'run away' from the burden God had placed upon me, He refused to let me escape from His assignment.

The Aftermath

This incident left me feeling even weaker than I had been before it came upon me. My long-term health problems were still there, but this gruelling experience had increased my exhaustion to a whole new level. I didn't know that it was possible to be so exhausted but to still actually be alive. All I know is that I spent a lot of time sitting in the conservatory looking out of the window, deep in thought, and much of the time weeping silent tears for the dreadful state of the Church that God had shown me from His word.

I felt like the whole burden to wake the Church up was solely on me, and I was absolutely terrified. I mean, let's be honest... what church leader was going to listen to me, a housewife and mother, who spent most of her life at home, unable to even get to church each week?! The thought of ever getting heard by anyone was beyond my imagination! I felt that if I didn't get this message out there quickly to the Church all around the world, then if any individual churches were allowing sin to remain in their midst, their eternal state would be upon my head! (see Ezekiel 33). This dreadful foreboding weighed heavy upon my soul day after day, and night after night. How could God give me such a horrendous burden to bear? I couldn't possibly carry this weight and bear the eternal consequences of the Church not waking up!

It was then that I heard, in my spirit, the Lord whisper to me, in such gracious love, that it makes me weep even now, eight years later. I felt Him say,

*"My child, I didn't ask you to carry the weight of the unrepentant sins of the Church, and I have not asked you to bear the consequences if they fail to heed my warnings to repent. All I asked you to do was obey Me in writing down the message that I want the Church to hear, which I gave to them in the Bible, but which they choose to ignore. Your act of obedience is **your part** in sounding the Trumpet to warn them to wake up, even if no one ever listens. I can tell you now that most of them will **not** want to listen, hear or heed what I have asked you to write. A few will, and their lives will be transformed by it because it conforms to My holy word. It will catapult them out of their complacency in the same way that My intervention in your life did. But I am letting you know now that even if no one reads it, **you** will still hear my words "Well done, good and faithful servant". When I ask you to do something, and you obey, that is all I require of you. How people respond to what I have asked you to do is something that will be between them and Me on the Day of Judgement. I will not*

hold you to account for their scoffing and rejection of the works that I have empowered you to do for My purposes and for My glory. Be at peace My child."

All I can say is, what a relief that brought to my soul!

Dreams and Visions

But before even hearing the word, "wake up church!", something else was happening to me, which went on for four years, crossing over into the writing and publishing of that book.

In 2008, I had begun to have very strange and vivid dreams which seemed so real that, as soon as I woke up, I thought that the events in the dreams had actually happened. The dreams started out as infrequent occurrences, perhaps once a month, but soon increased to regular dreams two to three times each week, and they really shook me up and I would wake up in a panic. But as they increased in frequency, I began to realise that the Lord was giving me the dreams for a reason.

I can only describe these as 'End Times' dreams, because I discovered about two years later that the events and details in the dreams were identical to the End Times events that Jesus spoke about in the Gospels and in the Book of Revelation. I would like to add here that at that time of having these dreams from 2008 - 2012, even after all the years I had been a Christian, to my shame the Book of Revelation was not something I had read past the first few chapters. I had no knowledge of what the bulk of it contained. So, to be having End Times dreams for four years without any knowledge that that is what they were, was quite a shock, and felt quite ominous to say the least.

In each dream that I had, I was in the scene observing all the catastrophic events that were happening. Desperate, frantic people would rush up to me, begging me to explain to them what was happening on the earth, and why. They seemed to sense that somehow, I would be able to give them the answers. In every dream, I found that I was boldly warning people that the events they were witnessing and experiencing were the fulfilment of Bible prophecy concerning the events that would lead up to the Second Coming of Jesus Christ. This led on to me telling them that in order to be saved and to receive eternal life in the kingdom of heaven, they must believe that Jesus Christ is the Son of God, and He is the only One who can save them; and then they must confess and repent of their sins and live in obedience to His word.

I could not understand why I kept having so many of these dreams, and I asked the Lord, what was the purpose of me having these troubling dreams if I could not personally do anything about the outcome. I had to wait for four years for the answer. I was praying in my room one day, when again I heard some more powerful words.

This time I heard, 'The End of The World and What Jesus has to Say about It'.

At that very moment, I then understood that all the End Times dreams which the Lord had been giving to me for four years, were for this specific moment. And I knew, with what I am certain is a supernatural knowledge which I am unable to explain, that the Lord was compelling me to write another book, with the title being, *'The End of The World and What Jesus Has to Say About It'*.

I knew that this would be another book to wake up the slumbering Church, but this time about being watchful of the signs of the times, and to be alert and ready for Jesus' return, which He says will occur when we least expect it. The book was to also warn unbelievers of their catastrophic eternal destiny without Christ as their Saviour, but also to show them what they need to do to be saved and to escape the torment of eternity in hell.

So, the moment that the Lord spoke the title words, I began writing immediately, and it was published in 2014.

Interestingly, these dreams stopped abruptly the moment I started writing the book!

Anything Else Lord?!

Thinking that must **surely** be my lot in writing books for God, I settled back into my life as a housewife and mother.... but not for long!!

In August 2014, only two months after the release of the second book, I was again in prayer one morning. Whilst interceding over the escalating state of the Church since 2011, again the Lord invaded my life with yet another message which He wanted the Church to wake up to. The words I heard this time were, 'The Gospel of Deception'. Swiftly on the heels of these words came more words, 'Counterfeit Christianity and the Fate of Its Followers'. Again, I knew that this was to be a book, but this time, like the first book, I did not know what to write. I was clueless to what 'gospels of deception' were, or what the Lord meant about counterfeit Christianity.

I knew that Paul mentioned 'other gospels' in Galatians 1:6-8, but I didn't think that such a thing would be something the Lord would bother me with. But clearly, He did want to bother me with it, and so I knew I had to wait on the Lord for the message, but I was now beginning to learn that I did not need to get frustrated with any delay. I knew that I could just go about my daily life and not have a melt-down during the period of waiting!

During 2014, my parents had moved back to the area where I lived, so I spent my time trying to be of help where I could in the first few months of their arrival. The book writing took a back seat, and I decided that I would start it again in the new year of 2015.

Little did I know what was to happen...

On January 17th 2015, my father collapsed and died very suddenly, and without any warning. My whole life was catapulted into a realm I had never experienced. It took two years for me to surface from this 'valley of the shadow of death'. I knew the book had to be written but I was not in a place for those two years to be able to sit down and write anything; and as for hearing from God, well… my ears were just not open to listening.

Get on With It!

I usually have a specific time of prayer on each New Year's Eve, to seek the Lord for the year ahead. On December 31st 2016, whilst I was praying, I heard Him say to me, "Get on with it!" I knew that God was referring to the writing of the third book, but how could I get on with writing it when God hadn't even revealed to me what He wanted to say about 'Gospels of Deception' and 'Counterfeit Christianity'? I didn't know where to start! I had a few scraps of paper on which I had written a few scribbled notes back in August 2014, but that was all! I felt God say to me, "Type up those notes, and then I will give you the rest of the message"!

I have to say I was rather anxious about this, but I dutifully obeyed God's instructions, and I sat at my computer and typed up all the notes from the scraps of paper. I then said to God, "Okay Lord, I have done that. Now what?"

I sat there for a few minutes…waiting on the Lord.

A Supernatural Download!

Then suddenly… my fingers started to fly around the keyboard so fast that they ached from trying to type at the speed of the words going around in my head! It was as if the Lord was downloading the message into my head in sentences, for me to type! I was completely staggered at what was happening! I typed and typed and typed for hours on end, day after day, with no foreknowledge of what I was going to type! I just typed what came out of the end of my fingers! It was a really strange experience, but also exciting to discover what the Lord wanted to say as I was typing it!

Some people reading this may find this all very bizarre and may even be uncomfortable with it, but let me just say to you, if you find it bizarre and uncomfortable, imagine how I felt with it all happening to me! I could have resisted it and not obeyed what I knew God was telling me to do, simply because it seemed to be a very illogical thing to do. When we are faced with such a situation, we either obey it, or rebel against it. Having experienced God do some strange things in my life with the writing of my first two books, I was not about to disobey Him simply because He wanted to use another strange method to fulfil it. All I knew was that with each book, He was using methods that would stretch my faith and my trust in Him. With each book, He wanted to show me that the work was from Him, and in order to do this, He had to use methods that were beyond my own ability to comprehend or achieve. When I think back on how He has done this for those three books, it just blows me away!

That third book, *The Gospel of Deception – Counterfeit Christianity and the Fate of Its Followers* was published in October 2017.

God's Purpose in the Pain

During the writing of all three books, my body has struggled daily with unrelenting pain and weariness. In the natural, I could not have written three books on such challenging subjects, let alone actually type them up into manuscripts; not feeling the way that I do every day. This is why I know that the work He has given me to do is most certainly from Him, and not of my own doing. He seems to give me the strength to sit at my computer and type for hours and hours, even suffering from EMF sensitivity, when all I really want to do is lay flat in my bed because of the pain and weakness in my muscles.

I feel certain that God has been and is still using my pain and suffering for His purposes and for His glory. In these years of isolation at home, I have begun to realise that writing all these books for God is the 'silent but powerful' ministry that He said would be my calling, when I was in my time of prayer, on our honeymoon. Books are vessels that contain messages in a silent form. When they contain the truth of the word of God, they can become a very powerful message to the reader, reigniting in them a hunger and thirst to read the Bible again, which can transform them and change the course of their life forever.

In my solitude, God has got me alone and got my attention, and I want to redeem that time for Him. I have no desire anymore to waste that time on doing things for my own pleasure. I don't want to do anything else except be in His presence. Whilst I have not liked being in so much pain for so long, it has enabled Him to use me for His purpose in ways that still astound me to this day. I don't take any credit for this because it is **all** His doing.

The Future?

As I type these words to close this final chapter of this fourth book, I am still in pain, and feel even weaker than I have in all the previous years. At times the pain is so all-consuming that I am unable to stand upright for very long, and have to rest in bed for an hour or so. There have been, and still are many times, when I feel so low and in despair at the unrelenting struggle, wondering where God is; rather like the psalmist in this passage:

"O LORD, how long will you forget me? Forever? How long will you look the other way? How long must I struggle with anguish in my soul, with sorrow in my heart every day?" – Psalm 13:1-2

Yet I have accepted that God wants to use me **in** my pain. The silence of suffering has a way of riveting my soul to fulfilling the purposes of God. Walking on this painful path for so long has got me to the place where I now understand that I am not here on this planet for any other reason.

I also know and believe that God can just speak a word and heal me in an instant. I will always wait in hope for this to happen, but I will not let its tarrying cause me to lose my faith in Him. If God wants to use me in my pain until the day He calls me home, then I will trust Him in the journey. I will not let the words of others towards my continual suffering deter me from the path and the course that God has set before me. When such words come, my part is to pray that God will open their eyes to the multitude of ways that He uses His people for His purposes, whether that be in sickness or in health.

To those who say, "It is not God's will for you to suffer", the great Oswald Chambers, in his classic devotional, *My Utmost for His Highest*, says,

"How can we say, "It could never be God's will for me to be sick"? If it was God's will to bruise His own Son (Isaiah 53:10), why shouldn't He bruise you? What shines forth and reveals God in your life is not your relative consistency to an idea of what a saint should be, but your genuine, living relationship with Jesus Christ, and your unrestrained devotion to Him whether you are well or sick." [2]

God has shown me that He has a purpose in all the years of pain that He is taking me through. If my story has helped to encourage even one fellow believer in a similar situation, then this book has been worth all the painful struggle to write and publish.

I pray for every single believer who is struggling with a healing that hasn't happened. I share with you in your suffering. If your life is isolated at home, I encourage you to use the time in whatever way you feel able to, to do the work of the Lord. Do not beat yourself up over the fact that you can't get out to church services or witness to people. Some people, who are bed-ridden with chronic conditions, use much of their time interceding for others for hours each day. When we are in such circumstances, often this is the method God chooses to use in order to fulfil His purposes. We each have a work to do for God, and He will decide what that work is, and how it will be fulfilled in our lives. If it is to be done through sickness, the suffering is often very hard to bear, but in our weakness, God gives us His strength to do what would be impossible to accomplish in our own strength (see 2 Corinthians 12:9).

When we take up our cross and follow Jesus, we are joining ourselves to His sufferings.

"Then Jesus said to His disciples, **"If anyone wishes to follow Me** *[as My disciple],* **he must** *deny himself [set aside selfish interests], and* **take up his cross** *[expressing a willingness to endure whatever may* **come]** *and follow Me [believing in Me, conforming to My example in living and,* **if need be, suffering or perhaps dying because of faith in Me]."** *–* Matthew 16:24 AMP (author's emphasis)

When we endure and overcome all that is required of us in this life as we walk the difficult, narrow path that leads to eternal life, we will one day hear those words, "Well done, good and faithful servant" (see Matthew 25:21). At that moment, all the pain and suffering we have borne in our life for God's purposes and His glory will have been worth it. Every burden of suffering will vanish in the twinkling of an eye. If our healing doesn't happen here on earth, what a glorious day awaits us when we cross over from this earthly life into eternal life in heaven!

"He will wipe every tear from their eyes, and there will be no more death or sorrow or crying or pain. All these things are gone forever." – Revelation 21:4

Hold on to this promise, as it will most assuredly be fulfilled.

Epilogue

Let God be God

"For God alone my soul waits in silence and quietly submits to Him, for my hope is from Him. He only is my rock and my salvation; My fortress and my defense, I will not be shaken or discouraged."
Psalm 62:5-6 AMP

It is now time to bring this book to its final close.

My 27 years of being a follower of Christ has taught me that we must **let God be God**, in every area of our lives, including healing. My journey has shown me, without doubt, that we cannot demand God to do something for us that is not yet in His timing to do. We cannot just say a few spiritually-sounding words of prayer as though it is a 'magic wand', and expect every single person to be healed on the spot. God does not work like this. He has a purpose, a plan and a time for everything in our lives (see Ecclesiastes Chapter 3), including at what point some of our healings will occur. Some may be miraculous, and other healings He may take us on the long, slow route for His own purposes. Yet there are many healings that may **never** happen in our earthly life. No one knows why, and God does not seem to be in any hurry to explain…

It is at this point that we, as Christians, should **resist** any thought that the lack of healing in those whom we pray for is always the fault of the person who is suffering. It is not. Yes, there are times when healing doesn't manifest in a person's life, maybe because of unbelief, unrepentant sin or rebellion against His Holy word – God knows the full reasons of such cases. However, a huge number of healings that don't happen are actually part of God's plan, and God has a purpose in the pain.

If we are on a prayer ministry team, one thing that can be overlooked, in the area of praying for others, is the condition of our **own** life before God. It would be advisable to examine our lives and do a bit of spiritual 'house-cleaning' where necessary, putting things right and making sure that we are living godly lives in right-standing with Him. It is a hard truth that many healings may not happen in people's lives because **we** (the person praying for others) may be engaged in sin which we have not confessed and repented of. There could be many sufferers, all over the world, who have walked away from a prayer line unhealed because the person praying for them was living a life contrary to God's word. On the platform or in the pulpit they looked to be faithful, trustworthy people of integrity, but inside they may have had habitual, unconfessed sin in their hearts, and would not let the Holy Spirit convict them to come to repentance over their sins. People may not be getting healed because of sin in **our** lives, not theirs!

When healing doesn't happen after we have prayed for people, let our thoughts and actions towards them be pure and holy, gracious and loving, which honours God. Rather than silently judging them for not receiving their healing, instead, we can turn the prayer into one which praises Him for His goodness and faithfulness at all times, even when we don't understand why He has not healed them. Our prayer could be one which asks for God's strength for that person, enough for each day; one which encourages the person to keep seeking after God in the midst of their suffering. That would be such a prayer of blessing to pray over someone! I know that I would certainly feel uplifted after a prayer like that, in spite of my pain.

It is a fact of life that sometimes healing doesn't happen, and in many of those cases there is nothing that any human being can do about it. Those are the times that we really do need to step back from our roles as Christian leaders and get down on our knees and 'wash the disciples' feet'. In other words, come alongside those who still suffer, and offer comfort, understanding, practical support where needed, and a listening ear. Strengthen those who are weak by spending time with them, worshipping and sharing God's word together, and bringing Holy Communion to them in their times of isolation; with no further agenda to try and 'fix' them.

If we have prayed with them once, twice or even countless times over many years, yet their healing still remains unanswered, it is now time to leave the matter with God. We can continue to pray for them in the privacy of our own homes, but I believe that many who continue to suffer after many years of prayer can get to the point where they no longer want anyone to come to them directly to pray for them. They simply yearn for others to demonstrate love, respect and understanding towards them, to step back from their eagerness to make someone's healing happen, and to realise that it is time to **let God be God.**

Their healing will happen at His appointed time, either in this life, or the next. As ministers, and brothers and sisters in Christ, our job is to rejoice with them if their healing does happen in this life, but to bear their burdens with them if it doesn't.

If suffering remains with us as part of our journey with God in this earthly life, let us take comfort in what Paul wrote concerning the suffering we may have to bear as we carry out the ministry that God has called us to do. Paul looked with joy towards the reward that awaits all who are longing for Christ's appearing:

"Don't be afraid of suffering for the Lord. Work at telling others the Good News, and fully carry out the ministry God has given you...I have fought the good fight, I have finished the race, and I have remained faithful. And now the prize awaits me—the crown

of righteousness, which the Lord, the righteous Judge, will give me on the day of his return. **And the prize is not just for me but for all who eagerly look forward to his appearing.**" – 2 Timothy 4:5, 7-8 (author's emphasis)

No matter how weak our unhealed sufferings may make us feel, if our heart and soul yearn for God and long for Christ's appearing, causing us to live our daily lives for His glory, then we are faithful and genuine believers. The reasons for our suffering may be misunderstood by many in the Church, and some may inwardly (or outwardly) question our commitment. But we can rest in the knowledge that the Lord knows us by name, sees us as we are, and looks into our hearts, where no man can see.

Let us hear a final word from Ryle:

"Happy is he who, in spite of many infirmities, can say with Peter, 'Lord, thou knowest all things; thou knowest that I love thee.' (John 21:17)." [1]

To me, the ultimate purpose for the suffering I endure is for the testing of my love for God, and for His Son Jesus Christ. Every pain that I feel is the voice of Jesus saying to me, *"Michele, do you love Me?"* My actions of enduring and overcoming each daily physical battle is my response to Him saying, "Yes, Jesus, I love you."

I am still walking on this journey of suffering. The Lord is with me. My hand is in His hand, and where He leads, I will follow…

"If your faith remains strong, even while surrounded by life's difficulties, you will continue to experience the untold blessings of God! True happiness comes as you pass the test with faith, and receive the victorious crown of life promised to every lover of God!" – James 1:12 TPT

Glory be to God!

Addendum to Chapter 5

Salvation and Eternal Life

I feel compelled to write further on the digression I made in Chapter 5 (in the section sub-headed 'persecution').

To me, any Christian book should contain at least one paragraph giving the Gospel message; the critical point of this being the eternal destiny of those who reject God's word, and showing them the way of escape.

I am sure that most people know what happened to Adam and Eve when they disobeyed God, and sinned by following their alternative 'spiritual path' (i.e. the lie of Satan). God banished them from the Garden of Eden and posted angels at its gates to prevent them from ever entering it again. All humanity since the fall of Adam and Eve has been born with the inherent disposition of that **original sin of rebellion against God's word**. It is hardwired into our DNA.

Our eternal default position is that we will spend eternity in hell because we are all sinners. We all need to be saved in order to receive eternal life in God's kingdom. Salvation has only been made available to us through Jesus Christ:

*"And there is salvation in no one else; for there is **no other name** under heaven that has been given among people **by which we must be saved** [for God has provided the world no alternative for salvation]."* – Acts 4:12 AMP (author's emphasis)

There is no alternative, despite the multitudes of bogus and deceptive claims of other spiritual organisations the world has to offer. Any other spiritual path that offers salvation and eternal life by a means **other** than through faith in Jesus Christ, is an attempt to get into heaven through the wrong gate. Faith in Jesus Christ and what He has accomplished on the cross for our salvation, is our 'Entry Ticket' into heaven. Without faith in Jesus Christ **alone**, we will not be permitted entry, and we will weep in much sorrow for having trusted in the lies created by the alternative spiritual organisations of this world, which were dressed up to look like the truth. If your house was on fire and someone showed you that there was **only one way** to escape and save your life, why would you refuse to follow that person to safety? Why would you choose to remain in the fire trying to find another way to save yourself, risking being burned alive in the flames? God's way of salvation through faith in Jesus Christ is the only way of escape from the raging fires of hell.

We must believe in the only way of salvation that God has provided, as written in the Holy Bible, and nothing else. We must then repent of our sin, give our lives to Him, and live godly lives in obedience to His word. When we reject God's word, yet still profess to 'know God', we may find ourselves on the wrong side of the gate when the time comes for our soul to leave our body.

"Not everyone who says to me, 'Lord, Lord,' will enter the kingdom of heaven, but only the one who does the will of my Father who is in heaven." – Matthew 7:21 NIV

How do we know that we 'know God', and what is the 'will of the Father'? The passage below gives us the answer:

*"**And we can be sure that we know him if we obey his commandments. If someone claims, "I know God," but doesn't obey God's commandments, that person is a liar and is not living in the truth. But those who obey God's word truly show how completely they love him.** That is how we know we are living in him. Those who say they live in God should live their lives as Jesus did." –* 1 John 2:3-6 (author's emphasis)

The Amplified Bible puts that passage in a very powerful way, which should leave us without any doubt as to who truly are followers of Christ, and who are the ones who simply say they 'know God', but do not obey His word.

"And this is how we know [daily, by experience] that we have come to know Him [to understand Him and be more deeply acquainted with Him]: if we habitually keep [focused on His precepts and obey] His commandments (teachings). Whoever says, "I have come to know Him," but does not habitually keep [focused on His precepts and obey] His commandments (teachings), is a liar, and the truth [of the divine word] is not in him. But whoever habitually keeps His word and obeys His precepts [and treasures His message in its entirety], in him the love of God has truly been perfected [it is completed and has reached maturity]. By this we know [for certain] that we are in Him: whoever says he lives in Christ [that is, whoever says he has accepted Him as God and Savior] ought [as a moral obligation] to walk and conduct himself just as He walked and conducted Himself." – 1 John 2:3-6 AMP

According to God's word, those who say they 'know God' but do not obey His word, are not followers of Christ, despite however much they may profess to be. It is obedience to God's word that is the benchmark that reveals if someone is a true follower of Christ, or not. If we say that we know God, but do not obey His word, (i.e. we do not solely believe that His word is the only authority on salvation, and we pick and mix His word with a host of other teachings from other spiritual belief systems), may this revelation from the above scripture passage convict us to do all that is necessary to put the matter right, as a matter of urgency. Our eternal destiny depends upon it.

Notes

Chapter 5

1. A passage taken from the morning reading dated 24th February
    of *Daily Readings from All Four Gospels: For Morning and Evening*
    by J.C. Ryle
    EP BOOKS, 1st Floor Venture House, 6 Silver Court, Watchmead,
    Welwyn Garden City, UK, AL7 1TS
    Used by permission.

2. A passage taken from the morning reading dated 27th February
    of *Daily Readings from All Four Gospels: For Morning and Evening*
    by J.C. Ryle
    EP BOOKS, 1st Floor Venture House, 6 Silver Court, Watchmead,
    Welwyn Garden City, UK, AL7 1TS
    Used by permission.

3. A passage taken from the evening reading dated 24th February
    of *Daily Readings from All Four Gospels: For Morning and Evening*
    by J.C. Ryle
    EP BOOKS, 1st Floor Venture House, 6 Silver Court, Watchmead,
    Welwyn Garden City, UK, AL7 1TS
    Used by permission.

Chapter 6

1. Excerpt taken from page 184 of *Come Away My Beloved* by Frances
    J. Roberts
    Used by permission of Barbour Publishing, Inc., Uhrichsville,
    Ohio, USA.

2. An excerpt taken from the December 2nd entry of Oswald
    Chambers' *My Utmost for His Highest,* ed. James Reimann (Grand
    Rapids MI: Discovery House, 1992). Used by permission.

Epilogue

1. A passage taken from the evening reading dated 24th March of
   Daily Readings from All Four Gospels: For Morning and Evening by
   J.C. Ryle
   EP BOOKS, 1st Floor Venture House, 6 Silver Court, Watchmead,
   Welwyn Garden City, UK, AL7 1TS
   Used by permission.

Recommended Reading

1. *Unexpected Healing*
   Jennifer Rees Larcombe
   ISBN 978-0340556863

2. *The Year of The Lord's Favor - A Prophetic Message to America*
   Darren Hibbs
   ISBN 978-0988919518

3. *The Christian Book for Men – Biblical Solutions to the Battles Facing Men*
   Chris Neal
   ISBN 978-7194347212

4. *Rush of Heaven*
   Ema McKinley with Cheryl Ricker
   ISBN 978-0-310-33890-1

Contact the Author

Follow Michele on Twitter: @MicheleNealUK

Visit her website: www.michelenealuk.com

Other Books by the Author

Come on Church! Wake Up! – Sin Within the Church and What Jesus Has to Say About It

Paperback:
ISBN 978-1-62136-316-3

e-book:
ISBN 978-1-62136-315-6

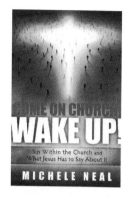

The End of The World and What Jesus Has to Say About It

Paperback:
ISBN 978-1-62136-742-0

e-book:
ISBN 978-1-62136-743-7

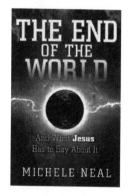

The Gospel of Deception – Counterfeit Christianity and the Fate of Its Followers

Paperback:
ISBN 978-1974387014

e-book:
ISBN 1974387011

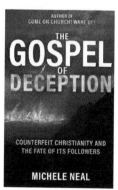

All books available from Amazon

Printed in Great Britain
by Amazon